SANS Step-by-Step Series

SECURING LINUX

A Survival Guide for Linux Security

Version 1.0

February 2003

David Koconis
Jim Murray
Jos Purvis
Darrin Wassom

Managing Editor: Barbara H. Rietveld
Publication Designer: José Ellauri
International Standard Book Number: 0-9724273-5-x
Library of Congress Control Number: 2003101190
Printed in the United States of America

It has been a real privilege to be part of the talented team of people who work with securing Linux on a daily basis and have labored long hours to compile this guide in a timely manner. It has not been easy, but they have done a great job at putting together a thorough and accurate step-by-step approach to securing Linux.

In our effort to include the best practices across the board, many technical reviews were done to ensure that, when put into practice, the ideas and examples in the Guide do work according to the text. As with any *inx variant OS, there are several ways to accomplish the same task. While most of them work and provide a similar outcome, we had to draw the line on what to include for the sake of making this a useful guide. If you have more efficient ways of dealing with issues discussed, please feel free to send them to me at linux-sbs@sans.org for possible inclusion in versions published at a later date. We concentrated on Red Hat 7.3 because it was the most widely used version while this Guide was being compiled and will be for some time until Red Hat 8.0 is better established. Remember that this is a guide, and should be used as such. Not everything included is for every system.

Education on the OS, applications and system usage are essential for a base in the security field. I strongly believe you should know **how** something affects the system, and not just how to "cut and paste" fixes. We have tried to explain the "why" behind all the recommendations in this Guide, and hope that every reader gains a little more knowledge about securing a Linux system.

Mitch Baker
Senior Systems/Security Administrator
Rose-Hulman Institute of Technology

SANS Institute enthusiastically applauds the work of these professionals and their willingness to share the lessons they have learned and the techniques they use.

AUTHORS

David Koconis, Dartmouth College
Jim Murray, NCCI Holdings, Inc.
Jos Purvis, Veritect
Darrin Wassom, Spectrum Health

EDITORS

Mitch Baker, Rose-Hulman Institute of Technology
Guy Bruneau, InfoPeople Security Solutions (IPSS)
John Moore, DigitalNet Government Solutions
Bill Stearns, SANS Institute

CONTRIBUTING REVIEWERS

Mark Austin, Cendant Mortgage
Benjamin Bergersen, www.Bergensen.org
David Bianco, Thomas Jefferson National Accelerator Facility
Matthew Brown, Chick-fil-a
Joel Burrow, Collegis at Valencia Community College
Richard Cassi, University of California, San Diego
Markus DeShon, SecureWorks, Inc.
Scotte Elliott, Ohio Legislative Information Systems
Diana Frederick
Kirk Greaser
Bob Hartwig, Zee Medical, Inc.
John P. Jenkinson, Science Applications International Corporation (SAIC)

Scott Johnson
Joseph Ledesma, County of Sacramento, CA
Rob McMillen, USMC
Brian Melcher
Russell Morrison, AXYS Environmental Consulting Ltd.
Drew Nall, SecureWorks, Inc.
Stephen Northcutt, SANS Institute
Jason Orme, Fermi National Accelerator Lab
Donald Pitts, Raytheon
Dave Taylor, Weber State University
Kevin Wilson, Systems Analyst

TABLE OF CONTENTS

LIST OF TABLES

1.1 SECURITY POLICIES

Security Policies are the blueprints used to build a security program. Your organization probably has a policy that states a system must be hardened before connecting it to the network. In this book, we will show you how to harden a Linux system, step by step, so that you can adhere to that policy. In very basic terms, Security Policies are the rules by which we secure environments. There are many types of security policies. These include:

- **Corporate Security Policy** – Defines overall security rules that apply to the entire corporation.
- **Remote Access Policy** – Defines rules for connecting to a company's network from a remote host.
- **Password Policy** – Defines rules for creating, changing and maintaining strong passwords.
- **Anti-Virus Policy** – Defines rules for the implementation and maintenance of an anti-virus program.
- **Acceptable Use Policy** – Defines rules for the acceptable use of corporate resources, such as Internet, e-mail, workstations, network, etc.

Samples of these policies can be found at http://www.sans.org/newlook/resources/policies/policies.htm

Your company may already have many of these policies implemented. If you are involved in writing security policies, there are some guidelines you should remember.

- **Security Policies should answer the Who, What, When, Where and Why of your objective.**
  Some elements of a security policy that help achieve this include a purpose, background, scope, action and responsibility. Guidelines, Standards and Procedure documents answer the question of **how** the policy will be implemented.

- **Security Policies should be clear and concise.**
  Security Policies are useless if they cannot be understood or contain the same number of pages as *War and Peace*.

- **Security Policies should be enforceable.**
  If your Senior Management will not follow the policy, you cannot expect the rest of your employees to. A classic example of this is an e-mail policy that forbids sending personal e-mail from work. The first time your CEO sends an e-mail to his wife, your policy became unenforceable.

1.2 DEFENSE-IN-DEPTH

In today's world, it is very rare to find instances of a single layer of protection. Homes have door and window locks, deadbolts, an alarm system, and fences around the yards. Cars have door locks, an alarm system that, in most cases, makes a loud noise and kills the ignition, and a steering wheel lock of some kind. In Information Security, this layered approach is commonly referred to as Defense-In-Depth.

Due to the large variety of attacks present today, Defense-In-Depth is necessary to properly secure systems. Some of the elements of Defense-In-Depth include:

- **BIOS Passwords** – This prevents an unauthorized individual from booting a system.
- **Physical Security** – An unauthorized individual should not be given physical access to the system(s). If they can remove the system from the building, they can put the hard drive(s) in a system they control.
- **Chassis Locks** – This prevents an unauthorized individual from gaining access to the internals of a system.
- **Firewalls** – This protects the system by only allowing access to those protocols we have defined in our security policies
- **Intrusion Detection** – This protects the system by watching for and alerting on known vulnerabilities.
- **File Integrity Software (Tripwire)** – This protects the system by comparing the signature of critical files to a database of known good signatures.
- **Logging** – This protects the system by recording identified critical events.
- **Baseline and Auditing** – This protects the system by taking a snapshot of the system before it goes on the network and comparing that snapshot to snapshots taken at a regular interval.

1.3 PASSWORD PROTECTION

Password protection is probably the most difficult security measure to enforce. It seems that no matter how many password restrictions we impose, the user community can find ways to undermine them. Users will try everything from writing down passwords to selecting one password, adding a number to the end and incrementing that number each time they are required to change their password. As security administrators there are some things we can do to help users understand the importance of password protection.

- **Security Awareness Programs** – Having a security awareness program will help users understand why we need security, and the implications of poor security management.
- **Balancing Password Length and Expiration** – Some companies require that the user change their password every month and have a 14-character password, while other companies require a five-character password while never requiring the user to change it. The first option is acceptable to the security professional, while the second option is usually what the user would like. If you want your users to practice good password management principles, you need to strike a balance between password length and expiration. In order to have the users remember a longer password, the expiration period may be extended. On the other hand, if the policy allows shorter passwords, more frequent password changes should be required.

1.4 DATA STEWARDSHIP

Data Stewardship deals with the classification and ownership of data. The data classification process usually starts with a risk analysis to determine which data are the most critical. The risk analysis is usually performed using the Threat/Vulnerability/Impact trifecta. Threat is the action taken against a system. Vulnerability is the weakness in a system that allows the Threat to occur. Impact is the expected loss should that Threat be realized. By determining which systems are the most vulnerable to threats and will cause the greatest impact to the company, a classification scheme can then be implemented to identify the most critical systems and data. The granularity of the classification scheme used is dependent on the type of organization and the data that it has. Government and financial institutions have a very granular classification scheme that may include as many as five to seven classification categories. Most organizations do not need that granularity and will typically only have two or three categories, which may include:

- **Public** – If the confidentiality, integrity or availability of this data were to be compromised, the impact to the company would be minimal or non-existent.
- **Internal-Use Only** – If the confidentiality, integrity or availability of this data were to be compromised, the impact to the company would be significant.
- **Confidential** – If the confidentiality, integrity or availability of this data were to be compromised, the impact to the company would be devastating.

In addition to properly classifying data, security roles and responsibilities should also be clearly identified. The following roles should be the minimum that are defined; however, other roles may exist depending on the organization:

- **Data Owner** – This individual is usually a Senior Manager or Executive. This is the individual who is ultimately responsible for the data and should be the one to make the final decisions regarding classification, access control and management of the data.
- **Data Guardian/Custodian** – This individual is usually assigned by the Data Owner and is responsible for the day to day management of the data. This includes backing up the data, restoring the data, and maintaining the data in accordance with the policies implemented by the data owner.
- **Data User** – This is the individual who uses the data as part of his regular duties and processes.

1.5 PATCHING/UPGRADES

Thanks to exploits like Code Red and Nimda, patching has become an obsession. Although patching is a necessary evil, it can be overdone. Some of the guidelines to remember when applying patches:

- **Review each patch for relevance** – If you are not running a service or application on your server, there is no need to apply a patch for that service or application.

- **Read the Release Notes** – It is understood that, as a rule, instructions are an annoyance. However when it comes to release notes, you need to read them to understand what the patch is going to do and how it is going to apply to your environment.
- **Always apply patches in a test environment first** – Unless you need practice in resume writing, it is a good practice to test your patches before you apply them to your production environment. The last thing you need is to apply a patch to a critical web server and bring the whole e-commerce site down.
- **Reaudit the system for unexpected changes** – When patches are applied, they can sometimes change system or configuration files back to the default settings. After applying patches to a system, the system should be reaudited against the last known good configuration for any unexpected changes.

1.6 BACKUP/RECOVERY PLAN

In the IT world, backup of systems is like brushing our teeth; we do it without even thinking about it. It has to be done so we do it. Because of the routine, we often do not consider the security implications around our backup procedures. Some security guidelines to remember:

- **Secure backup tapes** – Backup tapes are often the only way to restore systems after an incident.
- **Have a clearly documented backup plan** – Backup responsibilities usually lie with an operations center or with lower level IT people. Because these individuals rotate on a regular basis, it is necessary to have a clearly documented backup plan so that backup procedures are performed consistently.
- **Clearly label backup tapes** – Clearly labeling backup tapes will prevent restoring a system with a tape that was not from that system.
- **Store a copy of backup tapes offsite** – Offsite storage of backup tapes prevents against destruction by environmental disasters. It also helps to prevent against theft of backup tapes.
- **Verify backup tapes** – Periodically run verifications against backup tapes to ensure that backup software is functioning properly and what you intended to backup was actually backed up.
- **Test restore procedures periodically** – Testing restore procedures periodically will help eliminate surprises. You don't want to find out in the middle of a critical restore that you forgot something and have to start all over again.

1.7 BASELINES AND CONTROL AUDITS

One of SANS' mantras is "How can you properly secure your systems if you don't know what your systems are supposed to look like?" This is accomplished by establishing proper base-lining, change management and control audit procedures. Some guidelines to remember:

- **Take baselines of systems before installing on network** –A system becomes a target as soon as it is connected on a network. By performing a baseline of the system before it is on the network, you ensure that the baseline you have performed is clean.
- **Establish a documented, repeatable baseline procedure** – A baseline strategy cannot be effective if the same procedures are not used each time. This means that a baseline cannot be performed solely from memory. Checklists are an excellent form of documentation for a baseline procedure.

- **Implement a controlled change management program** – By implementing a controlled change management program, you will be able to accurately record what changes were authorized for each system. With this historical record you will know exactly what should and should not change on your systems from the baseline.
- **Perform control audits to protect against unauthorized changes** – Auditing systems on a regular basis performs two functions. First, it allows for the evaluation of the current system's state to the baseline. This ensures that you always know what state the system is in. Auditing also allows the tracking of all changes going through the change management program, and catching those changes that are not.

1.8 ACCOUNT MANAGEMENT

Account Management is also a critical piece of the security puzzle. There have been many instances where terminated employees were able to access systems long after they have been terminated by a company. Some important guidelines to remember:

- **Disable user accounts immediately after they leave the company.**
- **Periodically review and monitor user lists and groups for unauthorized changes** – This task should be a part of the base-lining and control audit procedures referenced in section 1.7.
- **Ensure that a user's rights are adjusted when they change departments or responsibilities** – If you have a user that moves from an Application Development role to a Support role, you do not want that user to continue to have access rights to the source code repository.

1.9 PHYSICAL SECURITY

Physical Security is just another step in the Defense-In-Depth methodology. Physical Security centers on protecting the system from physical and environmental threats. Some guidelines to remember:

- **Set BIOS passwords** – This helps to ensure that only administrators can change the hardware configuration of a system
- **Utilize cabinet locks** – Place critical systems in locked cabinets to protect them from unauthorized power down or unauthorized access to CD-ROM and floppy drives.
- **Ensure that badge readers or security cameras monitor access to servers** – This will help track an event should you have a security incident where the physical security is breached.
- **Educate mobile users on laptop security** – Teach mobile users how to utilize laptop locks. Also teach them proper transport techniques to use while traveling.

2.1 INSTALLATION GUIDELINES

2.1.1 Partitioning

Partitioning is probably the most widely discussed and debated topic when it comes to Linux configuration. There are many different opinions on how systems should be partitioned. Within Linux you can have many different partition types. The most popular of these types are:

/boot = Contains all files necessary for the boot process. This includes the kernel and any bootstrap files.

/home = Contains each individual users home directory

/usr = Contains those files which are shared across a system by multiple users

/var = Contains those files which are variable and dynamic by nature. This includes log files, spool files, scheduler files, and temporary files

/ = Contains those files necessary for system management when no other partitions are available.

/tmp = Contains temporary files.

swap = Contains the paging file for memory management

By default, Red Hat 7.3 partitions systems as follows:

Table 2-1. Red Hat 7.3 Partitioning Defaults

Workstation	Server	Laptop	Custom
swap = 2 X physical memory	swap = 2 X physical memory	swap = 2 X physical memory	swap = 2 X physical memory
/boot = 50 MB	/boot = 50 MB	/boot = 50 MB	/boot = 50 MB
/ = depends on disk space	/ = 384 MB	/ = depends on disk space	/ = depends on disk space
	/var = 256 MB		
	/usr = depends on disk space		
	/home = depends on disk space		

Partitioning will mitigate one specific type of attack, denial of service. There are attacks designed to fill up a temp directory or a spool directory. If your system files are on the same partition as the directory under attack, your system could be rendered unusable. A good partitioning strategy is to partition off those directories that are most likely to be filled up by an attacker. Typically this includes /var and /home. If you have a server being used for a specific purpose such as web, ftp, or e-mail, you may want to consider creating separate partitions for the application specific files as well.

2.1.2 GRUB/LILO

GRUB is the boot-loader of choice in Red Hat 7.3. One of the many advantages that GRUB has is that it simplifies the dual-boot process between Windows and Linux. Refer to Appendix C for more information on securing GRUB in a dual boot environment. As with LILO, there are many different kernel level commands that can be passed to GRUB and you want to make sure that only authorized users are able to perform those commands. This is accomplished by password protecting GRUB. During installation you will be presented with the opportunity to password protect GRUB. When you create a password for GRUB, make sure you do not use the same password that you use for the root account.

NOTE: GRUB stores the password in clear text by default. Once Red Hat is installed, you can modify the /etc/grub.conf file to store the password in MD5 format by performing the following steps.

Convert the GRUB password to MD5 Format.

```
$ /sbin/grub-md5-crypt
Password: (At this prompt enter the GRUB Password you created at installation and press enter)
$1$m0tLR/$HbgQzWuPw3pdgGeRFSPH8 (This is the MD5 hash of the password)
```

Edit the /etc/grub.conf file and replace the clear text password with the MD5 hash. (It is important for you to use the –MD5 option so that grub knows that the password entered in an MD5 format. If you do not use the –MD5 option, the password will actually be the MD5 Hash.)

```
$ su
# vi /etc/grub.conf
/etc/grub.conf

# grub.conf generated by anaconda
#
# Note that you do not have to rerun grub after making changes to this file
# NOTICE: You have a /boot partition. This means that
#    all kernel and initrd paths are relative to /boot/, eg.
#    root (hd0,0)
#    kernel /vmlinuz-version ro root=/dev/hda7
#    initrd /initrd-version.img
#boot=/dev/hda
default=0
```

```
timeout=10
splashimage=(hd0,1)/grub/splash.xpm.gz
password —md5 $1$m0tLR/$HbgQzWuPw3pdgGeRFSPH8
title Red Hat Linux (2.4.18-3)
    root (hd0,0)
    kernel /vmlinuz-2.4.18-3 ro root=/dev/hda7
    initrd /initrd-2.4.18-3.img
```

2.1.3 Firewall Configuration

At this point in the installation you are asked what you want your firewall configuration to be. There are three different options for a firewall configuration out of the box.

- **No Firewall** – This option allows complete access to your system and performs no security checking whatsoever. Only use this option if you are not connected to a network and plan to configure your own firewall setting before you connect to a network.

- **Medium** – This setting restricts access to certain services on the system. Those services are:
  Services that utilize ports lower than 1023
  The NFS Server Port (2049)
  The local X Windows system display for remote X clients
  The X-font server port

- **High** – This setting is the most restrictive and denies all access except DNS, DHCP and anything else explicitly allowed by you.

All of these settings can and should be customized further to fit your individual environment. If you are configuring your system while it is plugged into the network, you should use the High setting and customize it as necessary. You can refer to Section 2.2.6 in this guide for additional firewall configuration instructions.

2.1.4 Account/Authentication Configuration

During an installation, you need to create a root password and have an opportunity to add additional user accounts. At this point you need to make sure you select a secure root password. You should also add any additional management accounts you will need at this time. You should also ensure that you maintain the MD5 encryption on passwords as well as maintaining a shadow file to keep passwords in a separate file from the user names.

2.1.5 Package Installation

Package installation is another confusing topic when it comes to the installation of Linux. Most commercial Linux flavors, such as Red Hat, come with a large number of applications to choose from. Many of these applications perform the same functions but use different formats. When considering the security of a system, the most important thing to remember is, less is more. When selecting which packages to install, regardless of whether the system is a workstation or a server, avoid accepting the default. Take some time to go through all of the packages that are offered. Find out what those packages do and select only the packages needed and provide only the functionality needed. Do not install packages just because they are available. If you do not need a given package, do not install it.

2.2 NETWORK SECURITY

There are several kernel options in Red Hat Linux that can be configured to increase the overall network security. Beginning with version 7.0, the kernel can be modified by editing /etc/sysctl.conf and making any necessary changes. This file is loaded whenever the server reboots or an administrator manually restarts the network services. As with any changes to the system, it is highly recommended to make a backup of this file before proceeding with the changes listed below.

2.2.1 Network Parameter Modifications

Edit `/etc/sysctl.conf` to reflect the following changes:

```
net.ipv4.ip_forward = 0
net.ipv4.conf.all.accept_source_route = 0
net.ipv4.tcp_max_syn_backlog = 4096
net.ipv4.conf.all.rp_filter = 1
net.ipv4.tcp_syncookies = 1
net.ipv4.conf.all.send_redirects = 0
net.ipv4.conf.all.accept_redirects = 0
net.ipv4.conf.default.accept_redirects = 0
```

Save changes to `/etc/sysctl.conf` and perform the following functions:

```
[root] # chown root:root /etc/sysctl.conf
[root] # chmod 0600 /etc/sysctl.conf
[root] # /etc/rc.d/init.d/network restart
```

Brief examples of the changes made are outlined below. The appendix contains URLs that can be used to gain a further understanding of these defined parameters.

- `net.ipv4.ip_forward = 0` – This parameter disables IP Forwarding. **NOTE:** IP Forwarding should be enabled (net.ipv4.ip_forward = 1) if the server will be acting as a gateway or router.
- `net.ipv4.conf.all.accept_source_route = 0` – This parameter disables IP Source Routing.
- `net.ipv4.tcp_max_syn_backlog = 4096` – This parameter enables SYN flood protection.
- `net.ipv4.conf.all.rp_filter = 1` – This parameter enables IP Spoofing protection.
- `net.ipv4.tcp_syncookies = 1` – This parameter enables TCP SYN Flood protection.
- `net.ipv4.conf.all.send_redirects = 0` – This parameter disables the ability to send ICMP Redirects.
- `net.ipv4.conf.all.accept_redirects = 0` – This parameter disables ICMP Redirect acceptance.
- `net.ipv4.conf.default.accept_redirects = 0` – This is another parameter that disables ICMP Redirect acceptance.

2.2.2 Advanced Firewall Configuration

It is highly recommended to use IPTABLES for any type of advanced firewall configuration. Your particular needs will vary depending on your network and the types of services you want to have open. Providing examples for every scenario you may encounter is beyond the scope of this guide, but a few examples are provided in Appendix B. In addition, please utilize the sites listed below for a better understanding of IPTABLES and how it can be of benefit to you:

- http://www.iptables.org
- http://www.linux-firewall-tools.com/
- http://firestarter.sourceforge.net/
- http://www.fwbuilder.org/
- http://www.stearns.org/mason

2.3 ACCESS CONTROL

2.3.1 Disallow Remote Root Login

Under normal operating parameters, there should never be a need for the 'root' account to log on to a server remotely. Any actions requiring a direct log on to the system via 'root' should be restricted to the local console.

Edit `/etc/securetty` to reflect the following changes:

```
tty1
tty2
tty3
tty4
tty5
tty6
```

Save the changes and perform the following actions:

```
[root] # chown root:root /etc/securetty
[root] # chmod 400 /etc/securetty
```

2.3.2 Disable CTRL-ALT-Delete

For those machines with poor or non-existent physical security, it is highly recommended to disable the CTRL-ALT-Delete function that allows an attacker to shutdown the machine.

Edit `/etc/inittab` to comment out the following line:

```
# ca::ctrlaltdel:/sbin/shutdown -t3 -r now
```

Save the change and restart the service for it to take effect:

```
[root] # /sbin/init q
```

2.3.3 Warning Banners

It is a widely held belief that presenting some sort of statutory warning message at login time will assist the prosecution of trespassers of the computer system. Changing some of the login banners also has the additional benefit of hiding OS version information and other detailed system information that an attacker might find useful when targeting his attacks. Clearly, the organization's legal counsel should review the content of all such warnings before any changes are made to the banners.

Edit `/etc/motd, /etc/issue, and /etc/issue.net` to reflect the appropriate warning message for your organization and save the changes. An example follows:

```
This system is for authorized use only. All activity may be monitored and/or logged
```

An explanation of what each file does is listed below:

`/etc/motd` – This file displays the "message of the day" once the user has successfully logged into the system.
`/etc/issue` – This file is displayed to any user that is logging into the system locally.
`/etc/issue.net` – This file is displayed to those users logging in remotely via SSH, Telnet, or FTP.

NOTE: Earlier versions of Red Hat Linux contained commands in `/etc/rc.d/rc.local` that would overwrite `/etc/issue` and `/etc/issue.net` each time the system was booted. These commands are not present in the 7.3 release of Red Hat; therefore, modifying the files listed above should be sufficient in displaying the appropriate warning banner.

2.3.4 Password Protect Single-user Mode

Linux provides a mechanism for system maintenance via the "Single User Mode" which is typically started when the system is booting. This allows an attacker at the console to bypass any system protection and move into Run Level 1 as root. The ramifications are serious and it is necessary to password protect the single user mode to prevent this from happening.

Edit `/etc/inittab` to reflect the following change:

```
id:3:initdefault:
~~:S:wait:/sbin/sulogin
```

Save the changes and restart the service:

```
[root] # /sbin/init q
```

2.4 USER ACCOUNT SECURITY

The following steps should be taken to increase the security of user accounts on the system.

2.4.1 Password Aging

By default, Red Hat 7.3 requires users to change their password every 99999 days (i.e. never) and sets no minimum limit on how long a password must be kept before changing it. Issue the following command to set limits for all existing users whose ID is greater than 500, the default range for normal user accounts.

```
[root@localhost]# awk -F: '$3 >= 500 { system ("chage -M 180 -m 2 " $1) }' /etc/passwd
```

Change the following lines in the /etc/login.defs so newly created user accounts will inherit these values.

```
PASS_MAX_DAYS  99999 -> PASS_MAX_DAYS    180
PASS_MIN_DAYS  0       -> PASS_MIN_DAYS    2
```

2.4.2 Purging Unnecessary Accounts

Several unneeded user accounts are added to the system at the time of installation. For better system security, the number of users in the /etc/passwd file should be as small as required for the system to fulfill its mission. This will make it easier to detect any unauthorized additions of users. Before making any edits, copy the files to backup versions:

```
[root@localhost]#for file in /etc/{passwd,shadow,group} ; do /bin/cp -p $file $file.orig ; done
```

Remove accounts for unnecessary users using the following command

```
[root@localhost]# for user in uucp operator games gopher ; do /usr/sbin/userdel $user ; done
```

Remove unnecessary groups using the following command

```
[root@localhost]# for group in dip gopher games uucp; do /usr/sbin/groupdel $group ; done
```

Whenever users or groups are deleted, it is prudent to perform the following verification steps. First, to verify that no mistakes exist that will prevent users from logging in, run the following commands:

```
[root@localhost]# /usr/sbin/pwck
[root@localhost]# /usr/sbin/grpck
```

`conf.all.send_redirect`The pwck and grpck command verify, respectively, that the /etc/passwd and /etc/group files are properly formatted and have valid data in each field. Second, to verify that files previously owned by the deleted users or groups are assigned to the root user, issue the following commands:

```
[root@localhost]# /usr/sbin/find / -nouser -exec /bin/chown root {} \;
[root@localhost]# /usr/sbin/find / -nogroup -exec /bin/chgrp root {} \;
```

2.4.3 Locking System Accounts

Some user accounts are only used by a system service or daemon and never require interactive login. For increased security, the ability to interactively log in should be disabled for these accounts. Issue the following command, which assigns an invalid shell to the accounts (i.e., /del/null), to make sure they are locked.

```
[root@localhost]# for user in bin daemon adm ftp sync lp mail news nobody ; do /usr/sbin/usermod -L -s /dev/null $user ; done
```

2.4.4 Verify No Accounts Have Empty Passwords

Accounts with empty passwords pose a grave security risk to the system because all that is needed to login to such an account is knowledge of the login name. These accounts can be easily detected by checking to see if the second field of the /etc/shadow file is blank. Issue the following command:

```
[root@localhost]# awk -F: '($2 == "") { print $1 }' /etc/shadow
```

If no login names are printed, all is well. If any login names are printed, add a password for the user or lock/delete the account.

2.4.5 Tighten default umask

The umask for a user determines permissions on any new files created by the user. As installed, the umask for normal user accounts (defined as ones where the user name is the same as the group name) with user id greater than 99 is 002 (i.e. rw-rw-r— for files and rwxrwxr-x for directories). For other users, including the root user, it is 022 (i.e. rw-r—r— for files and rwxr-xr-x for directories).

For tighter security, the default umask for the root user should not result in creation of group and world readable files and directories. The default umask for normal users should not result in the creation of world readable files. Edit the lines in the /etc/bashrc and /etc/csh.cshrc files:

Change: umask 022   ->   umask 077
           umask 002   ->   umask 007

Caveat: Some rpm packages assume that the default umask will be 022 for the root user. Changing it to 077, as recommended here, will occasionally result in warning messages during installation or upgrade of these packages.

2.4.6 Miscellaneous Account Limits

The Pluggable Authentication Module (PAM) for Linux package enables enforcement of many different types of control over user accounts. Configuration files are located in the /etc/security directory. The configuration file regulating system resource usage is limits.conf and it is discussed in the next section. The configuration file regulating from where authorized user logins may originate is access.conf, and the one regulating at what time of day authorized logins may occur is time.conf . Default versions of the aforementioned three files are included in Appendix B. Each one contains comments that include implementation instructions with usage examples.

2.4.6.1 System Resources Usage (from Bastille)

To prevent individual users from consuming too many system resources, edit the /etc/security/limits.conf file so that core files will not be created (see note below), individual file sizes are limited to 100 MB, and a user can only have 150 concurrent processes running.

Add the lines:

```
* hard      core    0
* hard      fsize   102400
* hard      nproc   150
```

NOTE: For workstations used for software development, the information contained in core files is very valuable in tracking down bugs in code. Either do not include the line or change the word "hard" to "soft" so developers can manually raise the limit when needed.

2.5 SECURING (DISABLING) SERVICES

The number of services that should be listening for connections from the network depends on the type of system (i.e. workstation or server) and its mission (i.e. production web server, anonymous ftp server, development workstation etc.). However, the most secure stance for any given system is to only enable services that are required for the system to fulfill its mission and restrict access to only those whose job description requires it.

2.5.1 Identify Services That Are Configured to Start

The command-line tool chkconfig can be used to show the current configuration state for all run-level services. Two graphical front-end tools may be used to investigate status of services: ntsysv (requires newt package be installed) or serviceconf (requires Xfree86, gtk, and python packages be installed). Issue the following command to show the services that are currently configured to start when the system boots:

```
[root@localhost]# /sbin/chkconfig —list | grep -e "\(:.*on\|xinetd based\)"
keytable  0:off 1:on 2:on 3:on 4:on 5:on 6:off
syslog    0:off 1:off 2:on 3:on 4:on 5:on 6:off
...
xinetd    0:off 1:off 2:off 3:on 4:on 5:on 6:off
netfs     0:off 1:off 2:on 3:on 4:on 5:on 6:off
xinetd based services:
  wu-ftpd:  on
```

2.5.2 Create a List of Services That <u>Should Be</u> Started

Some or all of the services described below may appear in the output from the previous chkconfig command.

2.5.2.1 Independent Services

The list of services that should be run for every system is short. They are summarized in the table below:

Table 2.2. Services That Should Be Run

Service Name	What it does (see /etc/init.d/servicename)
keytable	Loads keyboard map for the system
syslog	Activates daemon that other daemons use for logging messages
network	Starts network interfaces
random	Increases quality of random number generation (important for applications encrypting network data)
crond	Enables cron daemon used for scheduling jobs
anacron	Manages execution of cron jobs that should have run during system downtime
iptables	Loads the iptables host-based firewall (if configured – see section 2.2.3)
ntpd	Controls system clock synchronization

2.5.2.1.1 gpm

Adds mouse support for the console mode text-based applications. If this is a workstation and X-Windows is installed, then this service should be off and the rpm package (*gpm*) can safely be removed. If this is a server without X-Windows and mouse support is desired at the console, this service should be on.

2.5.2.1.2 sshd (http://www.openssh.org/portable.html)

The sshd service encrypts all network communication and provides interactive shell and file transfer access for remote users. Note that the sshd service is NOT required by local users when making outbound connections from this system to another system with the ssh or scp commands. If users will need to access the system remotely, the sshd service should be configured ON so it will start when the system boots.

2.5.2.1.3 kudzu

The kudzu service enables automatic detection and configuration of system hardware changes. If configured to start, it will probe the system for hardware changes every time the system boots. If hardware changes occur only infrequently, then the service should be off. Note that kudzu can be manually started anytime to detect new hardware using the following command:

```
[root@localhost]# /etc/init.d/kudzu start
```

2.5.2.1.4 xinetd (http://www.xinetd.org)

The xinetd service manages the operation and start-up of many familiar services (see next section). If none of the services controlled by xinetd need to be turned on, the xinetd service should be off and the rpm package (xinetd) can safely be removed. Note that this service should probably be off for most workstations.

2.5.2.2 xinetd-Based Services

2.5.2.2.1 telnet

The telnet service provides remote shell access to a system without verifying the identity of the originating host or encrypting the data sent across the network. The service is inherently insecure and should not be used for connections across the Internet. Telnet should be off and the rpm package (telnet-server) can safely be removed. Note that users may still use the telnet client to make outbound connections even if the service is disabled.

2.5.2.2.2 wu-ftpd (http://www.wu-ftpd.org)

The wu-ftpd provides file transfer protocol service for remote users to transfer files to the system without verifying the identity of the originating host or encrypting the data sent across the network. The service is inherently insecure and, in general, should not be used for connections across the Internet. The primary exception is anonymous ftp servers commonly used for distribution of software source code and patches. Unless the system is an ftp server, wu-ftpd should be off and the rpm packages (wu-ftpd and anonftp) can safely be removed.

2.5.2.2.3 rlogin, rsh, rexec (The Berkeley r-services)

All of these services originating from BSD UNIX support weak IP based authentication and transmit data across the network as clear text (*i.e.* unencrypted). Note that this includes user login names and passwords. SSH was designed to duplicate the functionality provided by these services and can be configured to replace them in a way that is transparent for the system's users. These services should be off and the corresponding rpm package (rsh-server) can safely be removed.

2.5.2.2.4 snmpd - Simple Network Management Protocol daemon (http://www.snmplink.org)

The snmpd service is used to communicate with network management software. If there is no need for the system to cooperate with centralized network monitoring applications, the service should be off and the rpm package (snmpd) can safely be removed.

If the service is on, be sure to review the `/etc/snmpd/snmpd.conf` file. Settings in the file control who has access to the snmpd agent and what level of information the agent will provide. See the snmpd.conf(5) man page for more information.

2.5.2.2.5 tftp - Trivial File Transfer Protocol

The tftp service enables file transfers without any authentication credentials. The most common use of this protocol is by network devices that need to download configuration files from the network during their boot sequence. Unless the system is a boot server, tftp should be off and the rpm package (tftp-server) can safely be removed.

2.5.3 Disable and Remove Services That <u>Should Not</u> be Started

Any service that is not needed should be stopped and configured not to start on boot using the following commands:

```
[root@localhost]# /etc/init.d/servicename stop
[root@localhost]# /sbin/chkconfig —level 0123456 servicename off
```

In the commands, replace *servicename* with the name of a service shown in the leftmost column of the list output above (e.g. netfs or wu-ftpd). Repeat the command for each service.

The rpm package corresponding to the service should be removed using the command:

```
[root@localhost]# /bin/rpm -e packagename
```

In the command, replace *packagename* with the name of the rpm package to which the service belongs.

The package owning a given file can be determined with the following command:

```
[root@localhost]# rpm -qf /etc/init.d/servicename
```

2.5.4 [Optional] Verify Configuration of Run-Level Services
Repeat Step 2.5.1 and verify that the list of services that are configured to be on matches the list expected for the system.

2.5.5 Configure Access to Any Enabled Services

2.5.5.1 TCP Wrappers (ftp://ftp.porcupine.org/pub/security/index.html)
Access control to services compiled with TCP wrappers support is implemented by the /etc/hosts.allow and /etc/hosts.deny files. When a connection attempt is made, the hosts.allow file is checked. If a line is matched, the connection is allowed. Then the hosts.deny file is consulted, if a line is matched, the connection is denied. If no matches have occurred in either file, the connection is allowed.

2.5.5.1.1 Create Authorized Use Only Banners
If configured as described below, TCP wrappers will display a warning banner to any user attempting to connect to a service it monitors. The following set of commands generate the directory /etc/banners, and the files therein contain warning banner text for each service. In this example, the banner text is "Use of this system is restricted to authorized users." Note that exact wording of a warning banner is site specific; however, it should at least emphasize that the use of the system is restricted to authorized persons and that consent to monitor activities is implied by logging in to the system.

```
[root@localhost]# /bin/mkdir -p /etc/banners
[root@localhost]# /bin/echo "Use of this system is restricted to authorized users" > /etc/banners/
prototype
```

```
[root@localhost]# cd /etc/banners ; /usr/bin/make -f /usr/share/doc/tcp_wrappers-7.6/Banners.Makefile
```

2.5.5.1.2 Deny Everything Except What is Explicitly Allowed

In order to implement the security best practice stance of deny everything except what is explicitly allowed, issue the following command.

```
[root@localhost]# echo 'ALL: ALL: spawn (/bin/echo -e `/bin/date`"\n%c attempted connection to %s
and was denied"\
> | /bin/mail -s "Connection attempt to %s" root) &' > /etc/hosts.deny
```

Any connection attempt not listed in the hosts.allow file will be denied, a message will be logged to the syslog auth facility, and an email will be sent to root.

2.5.5.1.3 Allow Access to Those Who Require It

Edit the hosts.allow file and add a line for each service to which access should be allowed. A few examples are shown below (See the man pages for hosts.allow for more detail).

```
ALL: LOCAL : banners /etc/banners        # All services from local clients (hostnames with no ".")
sshd: 10.1.1.0/255.255.254.0 : banners /etc/banners # SSH connections from host IP addresses
between 10.1.1.0 and 10.1.2.0
```

2.5.5.2 xinetd

If xinetd has been disabled or removed (typically the case for workstations), this step should be skipped.

The xinetd service provides access control to the services that it manages. There should be one file in the /etc/xinetd.d directory for each service. To control access to a service, find the file with the service name and add the following line somewhere between the start and end bracket.

```
only_from =   10.1.1.0/23      # allow connections from host IP addresses between 10.1.1.0 and 10.1.2.0
```

2.5.6 (Servers Only) Disable X Windows

Server systems that do not usually have operators working from the console should not run the X Windows service. Issue the following command to configure the system to boot to run level 3 (multi-user mode with no X) instead of run level 5 (multi-user mode with X) and save the original /etc/inittab as /etc/inittab.bak

```
[root@localhost]# /usr/bin/perl -p -i.bak -e 's/id:5:init/id:3:init/' /etc/inittab
```

2.6 APPLYING UPDATES AND PATCHES

It is highly recommended that you configure the system to automatically check for availability of updated RPM packages. This will increase the likelihood that you will be able to patch the system and close any security holes that have been discovered before someone with malicious intent can use them to compromise the integrity of your system or data.

2.6.1 Up2date (http://www.redhat.com/docs/manuals/RHNetwork/ref-guide/)

For Red Hat 7.3, automatic checking for security updates is controlled by the Red Hat Network Daemon rhnsd. By default, the daemon will attempt to connect to a Red Hat server every 120 minutes to check for available package updates, download and install any updates for packages that are properly signed and are already installed on the system (except those whose name starts with the string "kernel"), then email the root user with results. Note that the use of the up2date service that exceeds one user with one system requires payment of a subscription fee.

2.6.1.1 Register the System with the Red Hat Network

The following command starts the Red Hat Network registration client and initiates the process of creating a system profile for the up2date service. The client prompts the user to create an account (i.e., username and password combination), then probes the system for the Red Hat version, hostname, IP address, CPU information, RAM, PCI devices, disk sizes, and mount points.

```
[root@localhost]# /usr/sbin/rhn_register
```

2.6.1.2 Verify Set-up by Manually Checking for Updates

Once the system is registered and the profile has been created, run the following commands:

```
[root@localhost]# /usr/sbin/up2date —nox -p
[root@localhost]# /usr/sbin/up2date —nox -u
```

The first command will update the packages associated with the system profile on the Red Hat Network, and the second will download and install the package updates for the system.

2.6.1.3 Ensure That the rhnsd Is Configured to Start When the System Boots

```
[root@localhost]# /sbin/chkconfig rhnsd on
[root@localhost]# /etc/init.d/rhnsd start
```

2.6.2 autorpm (http://www.autorpm.org/)

Autorpm is a viable, free alternative to up2date. It is written in PERL and can be run in interactive mode, passed command-line options, or called directly from a script. The default installation will check a Red Hat mirror site daily, download any rpm that is an updated version of one that is on the system (ignoring packages starting with the string "kernel-"), check the package signature, and email the root user with results. Although autorpm can be configured to automatically install rpm updates, by default none will be installed without user interaction.

2.6.2.1 Download and Install the Latest Stable Binary RPM

The latest stable rpm package for autorpm (2.9.3 at the time of this writing) can be downloaded from http://www.autorpm.org/tabs/download/. Once the package has been downloaded, install it using the following command:

```
[root@localhost]# /bin/rpm -i autorpm-2.9.3-1.noarch.rpm
```

2.6.2.2 Modify the */etc/autorpm.d/redhat-updates.conf* file

By default, rpm packages that fail the signature check will be placed in the interactive queue. To prevent these suspect rpm packages from getting accidentally installed later, add the following line to the *action(updated)* stanza after the line *PGP_Require(Yes);*:

```
PGP_Fail_Install(No);
```

By default, any updates for rpm packages that are on the mirror site, but do not have a corresponding earlier version already installed on the system will be added to the interactive queue. To prevent this from happening, find the *action(new)* stanza and change the line *Install(Interactive);* to *Install(No);*.

2.6.2.3 Verify Set-up by Manually Checking for Updates

Run the autorpm command with no arguments. The first time you run the command you will be offered a chance to see an explanation of how autorpm works and encouraged to download TermReadlineGnu. Accept the download. The package will be installed and autorpm will exit. Check for updates by issuing the command:

```
[root@localhost]# autorpm auto
```

You should see messages showing FTP connection attempts to a mirror site, and most likely, a list of package names for updates that are available. Updated packages (ones that have an earlier version already installed on the system) will be downloaded and their PGP signatures will be checked. When the prompt returns, issue the following command to install the packages:

```
[root@localhost]# autorpm "install all"
```

You should see messages indicating that the rpm packages are being installed, and if the installation is successful, that they are being deleted from the disk.

An entry in the /etc/cron.daily directory is added by default to enable daily checking for updates.

2.7 FILE SYSTEM SECURITY

2.7.1 Secure File System Mount Options

This section outlines edits that can be made to the /etc/fstab file to enhance the security of the system. Please note that the recommendations for mount options on the /usr and /home partitions should only be applied to systems where Server or Custom type was chosen during installation (see Section 2.1.1). This is because if Workstation or Laptop was selected, the /usr and /home directories will be part of the root partition (/), and the root partition must not be read-only, nodev, or nosuid.

Mount the /usr partition as read-only. Most of the executable commands on the system are located in the /usr filesystem. Mounting it as read-only is a good way to protect against Trojaned binaries being installed.

```
LABEL=/usr          /usr         ext3 ro          1 2
```

Note: The /usr file system will have to be remounted read-write before applying most rpm upgrades (including any scheduled to be applied by update agents like up2date or autorpm) with the following command:

```
[root@localhost]# mount -o remount,rw /usr
```

Once the installation is complete, the partition can be mounted read-only again with the following command:

```
[root@localhost]# mount -o remount,ro /usr
```

To prevent SUID or device files from being introduced to the system by removable media, add the nosuid and nodev options to the lines for all removable media (e.g. floppy, cdrom)

```
/dev/fd0        /mnt/floppy     ext3 nosuid,nodev    1 2
/dev/cdrom      /mnt/cdrom      ext3 nosuid,nodev    1 2
```

Lastly, the file system containing user home directories should also have the nosuid and nodev options set

```
LABEL=/home         /home        ext3 nosuid,nodev    1 2
```

2.7.2 Tighten Permissions on Files

2.7.2.1 Restrict Access to Administrative Utilities

Administrative utilities (*e.g.* chkconfig, traceroute, ifconfig, and iptables) reside in the /sbin and /usr/sbin directories. Under normal circumstances, unprivileged users should not need to execute any of these commands. Issue the following command to remove read, write and execute privileges for users that do not own the files (and do not belong to the groups that do own them) from all files in these directories.

```
[root@localhost]# /bin/chmod -R o-rwx /usr/sbin `ls /sbin/* | grep -v consoletype`
```

The consoletype utility is left out of the tightened file permissions because the files `/etc/profile.d/lang.sh` and `/etc/profile.d/lang.csh` call it, with the privileges of a normal user, to determine the type of console the user is logged into when starting a new shell.

2.7.3 SUID Permissions for Executable Programs

Other utilities that normal users can run reside in the /bin and /usr/bin directories. Some of these require SUID in order to work, for example, the passwd command needs to be able to write the updated password hash to the /etc/shadow file to which the user does not have read or write permission. However, on most files, the SUID and SGID permissions are an optional convenience, for example the ping command. To see a list of all the files with SUID or SGID permission use the following command:

```
[root@localhost]# /usr/bin/find /bin /usr/bin -type f \( -perm -04000 -o -perm -02000 \) -ls
```

Review the resulting list and remove the SUID or SGID permissions from files that do not require it by setting the permission on each of these files to 755. For example

```
[root@localhost]# /bin/chmod 755 /bin/mount /bin/umount /bin/ping /usr/bin/chfn /usr/bin/chsh /usr/bin/chage
```

2.7.4 Remove Compiler Packages (Servers and Workstations Not Used for Software Development)

Many exploits used by crackers are distributed as program source code and must be compiled on the target system before they can be used. If the compiler packages are removed from the system, then the cracker will have to upload a compiler along with the exploit source code before attempting to exploit the system. In addition to thwarting "script-kiddies", the increased activity required to install a compiler should facilitate detection of the unauthorized intrusion.

Issue the following command to remove:

```
[root@localhost]# /bin/rpm -e cpp gcc gcc-c++ gcc-g77
```

2.8 LOGGING

This section covers how to configure Red Hat 7.3 to increase the security of the subsystems related to logging. Steps in this section include configuration of what messages will be logged, where the messages will be sent, and how often the log files will be rotated. Additional related steps that will be presented are configuring automatic review of log files and synchronization of the system clock.

2.8.1 syslogd

Messages from daemon processes running on a Linux system are sent to the syslogd daemon. Each message has two properties, facility and level, that respectively describe what subsystem sent the message and how important the message is. How the logging daemon handles each message is determined by the /etc/syslog.conf file. Choices for handling messages include sending the message to a local log file, to the console or a local TTY, or to one or more currently logged in users, or to a remote log server.

Note that sending a copy of log messages to a remote log server helps to preserve a record of an intruder's activity when a system is compromised. While an intruder commonly erases or modifies local system logs to cover their tracks, they do not have the ability to do so on a remote syslog server unless they can break into that system as well.

2.8.1.1 Replace the Default Configuration File for the syslogd Daemon (/etc/syslog.conf) with a More Secure Configuration File

The syslog.conf in Appendix B ensures that important messages are recorded. The configuration also causes messages stored to the local file system to be segregated into subsystem specific log files. This makes each log file more readable and increases the chances that anomalies will be noticed when reviewing a log file.

2.8.1.2 Restart the syslogd and Ensure That It Is Configured to Run on Boot

Force the syslogd daemon to reload its configuration file:

```
[root@localhost]# /etc/init.d/syslogd restart
```

Make sure the syslogd is configured to start automatically on boot:

```
[root@localhost]# /sbin/chkconfig —level 2345 syslog on
```

2.8.1.3 [Optional] Verify the New Configuration

The logger utility installed with the util-linux package can be used to send a log message to an arbitrary facility and level. Use this feature to verify the configuration. For example, the command

```
[root@localhost]# /usr/bin/logger -p mail.info "Test mail log message"
```

should result in a line similar to the following being added to the /var/log/maillog

```
Aug 10 10:22:14 root: Test mail log message
```

Be aware that the implementation of logger does not enable sending messages to the kern facility.

2.8.2 logrotate.d

The /etc/logrotate.conf file contains the default options for rotation log files. These options may be overridden for a specific log file by modifying the files in the /etc/logrotate.d directory.

2.8.2.1 Edit the Default Configuration File for the logrotate Daemon (/etc/logrotate.conf) to Keep Log Information Longer

As installed, logs will be rotated weekly and saved for only four weeks. Edit the file /etc/logrotate.conf as shown in the table below so that important information about system events will be preserved longer. This will increase the likelihood that problems or suspected intrusions will be detected. Note that even though old logs will be compressed, a year's worth of log data may still be large. Be sure to monitor the available disk space for the partition where logs are being stored (typically /var).

Table 2-3. Default Configuration File for logrotate Daemon Settings

Default setting	Secure setting	Reason
weekly	monthly	These changes result in saving logs for a year instead of a month, providing longer accountability.
rotate 4	rotate 12	
#compress	compress	To conserve space, compress old logs

2.8.2.2 Update the Configuration File That Controls Rotation syslogd Files (/etc/logrotate.d/syslog)

The syslog.conf file installed in Step 2.8.1.1 will result in the creation of the additional log file /var/log/kernel for all systems. Furthermore, if any of the lines in that file specific to servers are uncommented, other log files will also be created. The name of all new log files must be added to the list of files at the beginning of /etc/logrotate.d/syslog so the new logs will also be rotated.

2.8.2.3 [Optional] Verify That Log Rotation Is Configured Properly

Use the '-f' flag with the logrotate command to force the log files to be rotated. New log files should be created and no errors should occur.

```
[root@localhost]# /usr/sbin/logrotate -f /etc/logrotate.conf
```

2.8.3 logwatch (http://www.logwatch.org)

The best logging configuration is rendered useless if the information in the logs is never reviewed. The logwatch application will automatically parse log files, attempt to remove entries that report normal activity, and send an alert email containing the unexpected entries. Edit the line in the file /etc/log.d/logwatch.conf line beginning with *MailTo* and change the user root to the email address of the person in charge of monitoring logs.

2.8.4 ntpd (http://www.cis.udel.edu/~ntp)

Configure the Network Time Protocol (ntp) server daemon to synchronize the system clock with three public NTP servers. This will enable a system administrator to reliably coordinate events from log files on this system with events from log files of other systems on the Internet.

2.8.4.1 Locate Three Public NTP Servers and Add Them to /etc/ntp.conf

Visit http://www.eecis.udel.edu/~mills/ntp/servers.html, select three public servers geographically nearby, note their IP addresses and obtain permission from their administrators. Edit the /etc/ntp.conf file and replace the line that begins "server 127.127…" with one line for each public server:

```
server 10.0.0.1    # IP address of public server 1
server 10.0.0.2    # IP address of public server 2
server 10.0.0.3    # IP address of public server 3
```

2.8.4.2 Restart the NTP Daemon and Ensure That It Is Configured to Run on Boot

Force the ntpd daemon to reload its configuration file:

```
[root@localhost]# /etc/init.d/ntpd restart
```

Make sure the ntpd is configured to start automatically on boot:

```
[root@localhost]# /sbin/chkconfig —level 2345 ntpd on
```

2.9 SCHEDULER SECURITY

2.9.1 Restricting *cron* and *at* Access

In the Linux world, *cron* and *at* are the applications of choice for scheduling. *Cron* is utilized when you need to have a particular job run on a regular basis at the same time interval each time. *At* is utilized when you want to schedule something to run once at a particular time. By default, access to *cron* and *at* are unrestricted. This means that all users have access to modify, add or delete jobs. *Cron* stores these scheduled jobs in user-specific files called crontabs. *Cron* periodically queries these crontab files for jobs to run. Jobs are run with the permissions of the user that scheduled the job. Some guidelines to consider when securing *cron* are:

- **Log all *Cron* jobs** – Red Hat is configured by default to send *cron* messages via the syslog function to /var/cron/log
- **Restrict access to *Cron* and *at*** – Only allow those users who have a need to run scheduled jobs access to *cron*. *Cron* regulates access through the /etc/cron.allow file. *At* regulates access through the /etc/at.allow file. Cron.allow and at.allow specify which users are explicitly permitted to schedule *cron* or *at* jobs, all other users will be denied access. If a cron.allow or at.allow file does not exist, *cron* and *at* will look for a cron.deny or at.deny file respectively. It is not necessary to use the cron.deny or at.deny file so do not create one. If neither of these files exist, *cron* will allow all users access to *cron*.

NOTE: Root will always have access to schedule jobs regardless of the contents of the cron.allow file.
To create the cron.allow file:

```
$su
# echo root > /etc/cron.allow
```

- **Ensure that programs executed by cron have the appropriate permissions** – Most system administrators love scripts. Scripts are excellent tools for automating many repetitive tasks that system administrators perform. By scheduling these scripts through cron, an administrator can perform a weekly or daily function automatically and gain valuable time. Some scripts require root permissions to run properly, so many times an administrator will run the script from root's crontab. This can create a security problem. Administrators usually create their scripts from their own accounts and those scripts are usually located in their home directories. This means that the permissions on the script are those of the administrator. If an attacker were to gain access to the administrators' own account, he would have access to modify the script. Since the script runs with root permissions, the attacker's commands would run as root. In order to prevent this, ensure that the user whose crontab is running the script or program also owns that script program.

3.1 WEB SECURITY

The web server installed with Red Hat 7.3 is apache (http://httpd.apache.org). The rpm packages distributed with the installation disk are vulnerable to multiple security issues (see https://rhn.redhat.com/errata/RHSA-2002-222.html). Be sure the latest updated packages (i.e., apache-1.3.27-2 as of 20-Dec-02) have been installed before proceeding.

3.1.1 Ensure Only Necessary Modules Are Installed

The httpd executable is compiled with Dynamic Shared Object (DSO) support to provide extensibility for plugging in many additional modules (e.g. SSL, PERL, DAV, etc.). Some of these modules are included with the base rpm package, but most of them are stand-alone packages having names beginning with the string "mod_" (e.g. mod_ssl, mod_perl, mod_dav). If the functionality provided by a module is not required, the module should be removed. A good candidate for removal is the Distributed Authoring and Version (DAV) module which enables modifications to files on the web server using the client's browser. Use the rpm command below to remove the DAV module package:

```
[root@localhost]# /bin/rpm -e mod_dav
```

3.1.2 Harden the Main Configuration File (/etc/httpd/conf/httpd.conf)

3.1.2.1 Comment Out Unused Modules

In order for the apache server to use the functionality provided by a module, the LoadModule and AddModule directives corresponding to the module must be present in the configuration file. For an additional layer of security, comment out (or remove) the pair of lines for each module that will not be used by the server. Some candidates for removal are:

Table 3-1. Candidate Modules for Commenting Out When Not Used

Module	Functionality provided	Comments
mod_autoindex	Automatic directory listings	Providing directory listings gives away too much information to potential crackers.
mod_include	Server Parsed Documents	If server side includes are not required by the website, it is safer to disable them.
mod_info	Server Configuration Information	Providing the server configuration information, just by visiting a URL, gives away too much information.
mod_status	Server Status Display	Providing the server status information, just by visiting a URL, gives away too much information.
mod_userdir	User Home Directories	Allows users to serve pages from a directory within their home directory. This introduces potential vulnerabilities if users are not web knowledgeable and careful.

Ref. 1: http://httpd.apache.org/docs/mod/

3.1.2.2 Tighten Default Directory Access Permissions

Change the <Directory /> stanza that controls the default access permissions.

Table 3-2. Modification of Default Directory Access Permissions

Original	Modified
<Directory />	<Directory />
Options FollowSymLinks	Options None
AllowOverride None	AllowOverride None
</Directory>	Order allow,deny
	Deny from all
	</Directory>

The original version allows symbolic links to be followed to anywhere on the file system. This increases the likelihood that files outside the document root might be shown to a visitor.

3.1.2.3 Document Root Access Permissions

Change the <Directory /var/www/html/> stanza that controls the access permissions to the web server document root.

Table 3-3. Modification of Default Root Access Permissions

Original	Modified
<Directory "/var/www/html">	<Directory /var/www/html>
Options Indexes FollowSymLinks	Options SymLinksIfOwnerMatch
AllowOverride None	AllowOverride None
Order allow,deny	Order allow,deny
Allow from all	Allow from all
</Directory>	</Directory>

The original version will show the visitor a directory listing for any directory in the document root without an index.html file (or other similar file defined by the *DirectoryIndex* directive). As mentioned in the previous step, this is too much information to give to a visitor. Another change is the use of the more restrictive *SymLinksIfOwnerMatch* option. Generally, all the files served by a web server are owned by the root user or web administrator. Therefore, this option prevents the server from following any links that may be created by other users to areas outside the DocumentRoot.

There is an option to consider (instead of *None*) for the *AllowOveride* directive. If many people have responsibility for access control to different directories under the web server document root, *AllowOveride AuthConfig* may be used instead. This will enable separate configuration of access control using a *.htaccess* (or a file name that matches the *AccessFileName* directive) file in each directory, instead of having to give everyone write permission to the main *httpd.conf* configuration file. The drawback is that it makes auditing access to the server more difficult, since there is more than one place to look.

3.1.2.4 Conceal Server Version Information

Apache is configured by default to add a signature to web pages that it dynamically generates (like default error pages). The signature potentially includes the server name, version number, and modules. The following directive, placed in httpd.conf, will prevent this signature from being displayed:

```
ServerSignature Off
```

In addition to the server signature, apache will provide a string in the HTTP header returned to clients requesting documents that contains the name, version, and modules that were loaded on start-up. The following directive will minimize the amount of information leaked.

```
ServerTokens Prod
```

Occasionally, the email address of the web server administrator is displayed on server-generated pages. Locate the directive below and change the email address to the address of the Webmaster.

```
ServerAdmin root@localhost
```

3.1.2.5 Disable cgi-bin Directory (if not used)

Probably the main vector used to attack web servers is a CGI program. If the web site hosted by the server does not host any CGI pages, comment out the following lines to disable CGI functionality and access to the cgi-bin directory:

```
LoadModule cgi_module    modules/mod_cgi.so
LoadModule env_module    modules/mod_env.so
AddModule mod_env.c
AddModule mod_cgi.c
ScriptAlias /cgi-bin/ "/var/www/cgi-bin/"
<Directory "/var/www/cgi-bin">
   AllowOverride None
```

```
Options None
  Order allow,deny
  Allow from all
</Directory>
```

3.1.3 Check Permissions on Files in the DocumentRoot

To help prevent defacements of web pages, the owner of the web server process should never have write permission to any file or directory where files reside that are served by the web server. The user and group that the web server process runs under are defined by the User and Group directive in the *httpd.conf* file, respectively. Run the following commands for all directories served by the web server to identify any files for which the owner of the web server process has write permission. For the best security, the output from the commands should be empty.

```
[root@localhost]# /usr/bin/find /var/www/html -user apache -perm +202 -exec ls - ld {} \;
[root@localhost]# /usr/bin/find /var/www/html -group apache -perm +022 - exec ls - ld {} \;
```

In these commands, the user and group are apache, as they are with the default installation. Also, for additional security, these commands can be combined into a script and run on a daily basis from a cron job so any changes to the files permissions will be promptly detected.

3.1.4 Encrypt Sensitive Traffic Using HTTPS

The Secure Sockets Layer (SSL) module enables the apache web server to use strong authentication for all client server communications. At a minimum, the https protocol requires that the server have an X.509 certificate for identification. Ideally, the certificate should be signed by a trusted third party who has taken the steps to verify that the server is actually being operated by who it claims to be. Optionally, the server may also require the client to provide a certificate.

The sample certificate installed with Red Hat 7.3 (/etc/httpd/conf/ssl.crt/server.crt) enables apache to start and function as an HTTPS server. However, if the server will be used to serve and handle sensitive data (e.g. for an e-Commerce web site), an authentic certificate should be created and signed by a trusted authority. See http://www.thawte.com/html/SUPPORT/server/softwaredocs/apachessl.html for details on how to create one.

3.1.5 Where to Find More Information

The GCUX practical entitled Securing Apache Step-by-Step (http://www.giac.org/practical/ryan_barnett_gcux.zip) written by Ryan Barnett is an excellent resource on these items and others related to the Apache server.

3.2 E-MAIL SECURITY

3.2.1 Sendmail

Sendmail is the default Mail Transfer Agent (MTA) supplied with Red Hat 7.3 and most other distributions of Linux. Red Hat 7.3 shipped with version 8.11.6 of sendmail and at the time of this writing, sendmail version 8.12.5 is the most current and stable version offered. It is advisable to upgrade to the current release of sendmail (http://www.sendmail.org) since it eliminates a theoretical buffer overflow vulnerability.

The configuration and operation of sendmail can be quite complicated in the hands of a beginner. It is highly recommended that anyone wishing to use the more advanced features of sendmail get a copy of Sendmail (commonly known as the "Bat Book") published by O'Reilly and Associates.

3.2.1.1 Disable Sendmail Daemon Mode on Workstation

Rarely should a workstation ever need to run a Mail Transfer Agent (MTA) in a daemon mode. Most organizations utilize a central mail gateway to route messages so the daemon can be safely disabled.

Edit `/etc/sysconfig/sendmail` to read:
DAEMON=no
QUEUE=15m

The QUEUE option controls how often sendmail will process the outgoing mail queue. In the example above, the queue is set to be processed every 15 minutes but this can be changed to suit individual needs to include seconds (s), minutes (m) or hours (h). Save the changes made to `/etc/sysconfig/sendmail` and restart the `sendmail` daemon:

```
[root] # /etc/rc.d/init.d/sendmail restart
```

3.2.1.2 Define SMTP Server for Mail Clients

Most Linux distributions include several command-line and GUI-based mail clients. Red Hat is no exception and ships with Pine, ELM, mail (AKA Mail), Mutt, Netscape and Mozilla just to name a few. While programs like PINE and ELM default to using sendmail locally, they can be configured to use an external MTA. However, the command-line application, mail, does not include an option to use an external MTA which makes changes to sendmail necessary to route messages through the central mail gateway.

3.2.1.2.1 Set Outbound SMTP Server for Sendmail

Option One:

Edit `/etc/mail/sendmail.mc` to read:
`define('SMART_HOST', 'your.mailserver.com')`

Keep in mind that 'your.mailserver.com' is the fully qualified domain name of the SMTP server for your organization. Generate a new `sendmail.cf` from the edited `sendmail.mc`:

```
[root] # m4 /etc/mail/sendmail.mc > /etc/sendmail.cf
```

Restart the sendmail daemon:

```
[root] # /etc/rc.d/init.d/sendmail restart
```

An alternate method is to edit `/etc/sendmail.cf` directly, but this is a generally discouraged practice. If, for some reason, using the m4 macro is not feasible, then edit `/etc/sendmail.cf` by looking for DS which can be located just after the "local info" heading. Change DS to read:

```
DSyour.mailserver.com
```

It may also be a good idea to edit the file to handle locally delivered mail by editing the entries that begin with "DR", "DH", and "DM" in `/etc/sendmail.cf`:

```
DRyour.mailserver.com
DHyour.mailserver.com
DMyour.mailserver.com
```

This will handle unqualified addresses (those without any @domain portion), local addresses (user@host without any domain information) and sets the masquerade address, respectively. Save `/etc/mail/sendmail.cf` and restart the daemon.

Option Two:

There exists a fairly unknown feature of sendmail written exclusively to handle the situation of a local workstation relaying all outbound messages through a central SMTP server. The feature is called the Null Client Macro File and allows an administrator to create an appropriate `sendmail.cf` without all the extra features normally present.

Create the `/etc/mail/null.mc` with the following lines:

```
OSTYPE ('linux')dnl
DOMAIN ('generic')dnl
FEATURE ('nullclient', 'your.mailserver.com')dnl
Define ('confPRIVACY_FLAGS', authwarnings, goaway, restrictmailq, restrictqrun')dnl
```

Generate a new `sendmail.cf` file by running the m4 macro and restart the `sendmail` daemon:

```
[root] # m4 /etc/mail/null.mc > /etc/sendmail.cf
[root] # /etc/rc.d/init.d/sendmail restart
```

3.2.1.2.2 Set Outbound SMTP Server for Mail Clients

As stated earlier, mail programs like Pine will default to using sendmail on the localhost for sending messages. However, Pine can be configured to utilize a remote SMTP server, if desired. You can set the SMTP server directly from the main menu by selecting "S" for setup, then "C" for config and then moving down to the field labeled `smtp-server`. Enter the hostname of the remote SMTP server here and save your changes. In addition to the `smtp-server` field, `personal-name` and `user-domain` can be edited to reflect individual needs.

The SMTP server is set in Netscape Messenger by selecting the `Edit -> Preferences...` dialog, selecting `Mail & Newsgroups -> Mail Servers` and placing the hostname of the SMTP server in the window under `Outgoing Mail Server`. Mozilla Mail is quite similar as are the countless GUI-based mail clients available for Linux. The general idea is to locate the mail preferences dialog and change the settings to reflect your environment.

3.2.1.3 Increase Privacy and Security of the Sendmail Daemon

Several options are available to increase the privacy and security posture of the sendmail daemon. By adding particular flags within `/etc/mail/sendmail.mc`, an administrator can restrict access to the mail queue, prevent certain commands from being issued by remote hosts or tell `sendmail` to insert special headers into a mail message. A summary of these flags is presented below but all the options presented below are explained in great detail in Chapter 34 of the Bat Book.

- `authwarnings` – this causes sendmail to insert special headers into the mail message that advise the recipient of reasons to suspect that the message may not be authentic.
- `goaway` – a shorthand way to set all of `authwarnings`, `noexpn`, `novrfy`, `needmailhelo`, `needexpnhelo` and `needvrfyhelo`.
- `restrictmailq` – this restricts who may examine the contents of the queue by allowing only those users who are in the same group as the group ownership of the mail queue to examine its contents.
- `restrictqrun` – this limits queue processing to root and the owner of the queue directory. Any non-privileged user who attempts to process the queue will get an error message stating they do not have permission to process the queue.

Edit the `'confPRIVACY_FLAGS'` section of `/etc/mail/sendmail.mc` to add the increased privacy and security flags as shown below:

```
Define ('confPRIVACY_FLAGS', authwarnings, goaway, restrictmailq, restrictqrun')dnl
```

Generate a new `sendmail.cf` file by running the m4 macro and restart the `sendmail` daemon:

```
[root] # m4 /etc/mail/sendmail.mc > /etc/sendmail.cf
[root] # /etc/rc.d/init.d/sendmail restart
```

3.2.1.4 Define Hosts Allowed to Relay Mail

Starting with version 8.9 of sendmail, relaying is prevented by default. This was done to prevent nefarious entities (e.g. Spammers) from being able to relay unsolicited email through a mail gateway that was not properly configured. Relaying is controlled through the access database located in /etc/mail/access and /etc/mail/access.db, respectively.

3.2.1.4.1 Check That the Access Database Is Active

To ensure `sendmail` has the ability to use the access database, check for the name of the database in `/etc/sendmail.cf`:

```
[root] # grep Kaccess /etc/sendmail.cf
Kaccess hash /etc/mail/access
```

If the line above isn't found, edit /etc/mail/sendmail.mc and add the following build macro:

FEATURE ('access_db')dnl

Generate a new `sendmail.cf` file by running the m4 macro and restart the `sendmail` daemon:

```
[root] # m4 /etc/mail/sendmail.mc > /etc/sendmail.cf
[root] # /etc/rc.d/init.d/sendmail restart
```

3.2.1.4.2 Create Access Database for Domains Allowed to Relay

The access database has a simple "key value" format that is used when configuring allowed relay domains for sendmail. The "key" is a fully qualified hostname, sub-domain, domain or network. The "value" is an action, REJECT, DISCARD, OK, RELAY or an arbitrary message. Only hosts or domains with the RELAY action defined are allowed to use the mail server as a mail relay. For example, if your domain is mailserver.com and our server is also handling mail for all hosts on the 192.168.x.x network, edit /etc/mail/access to read:

```
mailserver.com              RELAY
192.168                     RELAY
```

Save the changes to /etc/mail/access and use the makemap utility program to create the database map of this file and restart the sendmail daemon:

```
[root] # makemap hash /etc/mail/access.db < /etc/mail/access
[root] # /etc/rc.d/init.d/sendmail restart
```

Anytime information is modified in /etc/mail/access, it is important to run a new makemap command and restart the sendmail daemon so the changes will take effect. The example above is meant to illustrate simple usage of the access database. A more detailed explanation and advanced configurations can be found at: http://www.sendmail.org/tips/relaying.html

3.2.1.5 Set Domain Name Masquerading

Many organizations prefer to have uniform mail addresses for all employees, such as joeuser@mailserver.com. While some mail clients can be configured to use a specific domain, the administration of multiple mail clients in even a small environment can be tedious and cost prohibitive. Sendmail can be configured to rewrite the headers of all outbound messages so that they masquerade as a single domain name for the entire organization. To define the masquerade address, edit /etc/mail/sendmail.mc to reflect the following example:

```
MASQUERADE_AS('mailserver.com')dnl
FEATURE ('masquerade_entire_domain')dnl
FEATURE ('masquerade_envelope')dnl
```

Generate a new sendmail.cf file by running the m4 macro and restart the sendmail daemon:

```
[root] # m4 /etc/mail/sendmail.mc > /etc/sendmail.cf
[root] # /etc/rc.d/init.d/sendmail restart
```

3.2.1.6 Configure Sendmail to Use RBL Support

The Real-time Blackhole List, commonly referred to as RBL, is a DNS-based service that contains a database of suspected and known spammers. The m4 feature, dnsbl, allows sendmail to reference this database and automatically reject any messages originating from a domain listed by RBL. It should be noted that RBL is not an exact science and there are times when a domain you wish to communicate with has found itself listed by RBL. It can often prove difficult to get a domain removed so it is advised to use this feature with caution as it may cause a break in communication with legitimate domains. To add the feature to sendmail edit `/etc/mail/sendmail.mc` and add the following:

FEATURE ('dnsbl')dnl
Generate a new `sendmail.cf` file by running the m4 macro and restart the `sendmail` daemon:

```
[root] # m4 /etc/mail/sendmail.mc > /etc/sendmail.cf
[root] # /etc/rc.d/init.d/sendmail restart
```

3.2.1.7 Install an Alternative MTA

Several other mail transfer agents are available to replace sendmail. Three popular alternatives are Qmail (http://www.qmail.org) by Daniel Bernstein, Postfix (http://www.postfix.org) by Wietse Venema, and Exim (http://www.exim.org/) developed by the University of Cambridge. These MTA's were written with security in mind and generally considered to offer high performance. It is beyond the scope of this guide to give details on the installation and configuration of these alternatives but a wealth of information is available at their respective sites.

3.2.2 Secure the POP and IMAP Daemons

For mail servers that collect all incoming mail for an organization, a common means to deliver the mail to clients is for them to retrieve the mail using the Post Office Protocol (POP) or the Internet Message Access Protocol (IMAP). POP (also called POP3) is the older and less complicated of the two protocols, providing basic commands for authentication, retrieval and deletion of mail messages from the mail server. IMAP is more flexible and supports creating, deleting and renaming mail folders (mailboxes), searching, selective retrieval of message attributes and more.

3.2.2.1 Get the Latest Version of POP and IMAP Daemons

Unfortunately, many POP and IMAP daemon implementations have been plagued with vulnerabilities that lead to remote root compromises of mail servers on various platforms. There are several well-known exploit programs for cracking vulnerable Linux POP and IMAP daemons. It is generally considered a good practice to always use the most current and stable release of any daemons and this is no exception.

Most newer POP and IMAP daemons currently available will offer support for secure retrieval of messages. This is most commonly done with TLS/SSL that requires the use of OpenSSL and the creation of a certificate. Qpopper (http://www.eudora.com/qpopper/), for example, is a POP daemon that offers TLS/SSL. The website contains detailed instructions on how to accomplish this goal and is highly recommended.

3.2.2.2 Control Access to POP and IMAP with TCP Wrappers

POP/IMAP is traditionally run out of `xinetd`, so access control through TCP wrappers is easy to configure and adds an important element of security. Limit access to only those hosts that have a legitimate need for the service. For a central mail hub that holds mail for the entire mailserver.com domain and the 192.168.x.x network and delivers it to clients via POP3 or IMAP, edit `/etc/hosts.allow` to reflect the following changes:

```
ipop3d:         .mailserver.com        192.168.
imapd:          .mailserver.com        192.168.
```

3.3 FILE/PRINT SECURITY

3.3.1 Securing WuFTPd

Despite the recent increase in the deployed footprint of encrypted services such as SSH, FTP services are still sometimes necessary. Many clients (most notably certain Redmond-based operating systems) do not ship with an SSH client at all, which forces many administrators to accept the risks of cleartext FTP transfers. This section will discuss the configuration of the WUFTPd FTP server package shipped with Red Hat 7.3 for individual file transfers and anonymous file access in a secure manner.

Fortunately, the Washington University FTP daemon has gotten progressively more intelligent and useful over the years, and it now ships with a fairly secure default configuration from Red Hat. We'll edit this configuration file to enable secure user FTP sessions, then again for anonymous file transfers.

3.3.1.1 User File Transfers

By default, WUFTPd comes pre-configured to chroot all users into their home directories automatically. Even better, this action is done by the daemon and does not require creating additional binary or library directories on the server in order to function: it just works. In order to properly secure this, though, we'll need to tweak the main FTP configuration file, `/etc/ftpaccess`.

`/etc/ftpaccess` (Changes are marked in **bold**, comments in *italics*)

• Don't allow system accounts to login over FTP. *Comment out the right for the FTP user to login over FTP—that's only needed for anonymous transfers*

```
deny-uid %-99 %65534-
deny-gid %-99 %65534-
```

```
# allow-uid ftp
# allow-gid ftp
```

- Chroot all users by default

```
guestuser *
```

- List any users you wish to grant "real" privileges to (i.e. that should not be chrooted) here

```
realuser <ftp administrators, etc.>
```

- We don't need an explicit chroot group: all users will be chrooted!

```
# guestgroup ftpchroot
```

- Set your email address

```
email ftpadmin@ftpserver.mydomain.com
```

- Permit only 2 failed logins before terminating the session

```
loginfails 2
```

- Set the welcome message to something we can control and eliminate from directory listings

```
message /.ftpwelcome.msg          login
```

- Do not allow on-the-fly tarring and compressing

```
compress    no    all
tar         no    all
```

- Prevent certain actions by anonymous and/or guest users. Explicitly list permissions for everyone.

```
chmod       no    guest,anonymous
delete      no    anonymous
overwrite   no    anonymous
rename      no    anonymous
umask       no    real,guest,anonymous
delete      yes   real,guest
overwrite   yes   real,guest
rename      yes   real,guest
```

- Log commands and transfers to and from the server (this will not log passwords unless the user types one as a command by mistake).

```
log commands real,anonymous,guest
log transfers anonymous,guest,real inbound,outbound
```

- Mark certain files as non-retrievable

```
noretrieve .notar
noretrieve .ftpwelcome.msg
```

- Set a secure path filter to weed out evil files

```
path-filter guest,anonymous /etc/pathmsg ^[-A-Za-z0-9_\.]*$ ^\. ^-
```

- Shorten the greeting string so as not to provide the server version

  `greeting terse`
- Use secure default umasks for everyone

  `defumask 0377`

  `defumask 0177 real`

  `defumask 0133 guest`

Finally, we need to make some modifications to our users' home directories. Let's set up a user who will only be permitted to FTP files in and out of his directory, but nothing more.

```
useradd -d /home/user -s /sbin/nologin -m user
passwd user # Set the user's password
cd /home/user
cp /etc/issue.net /home/user/.ftpwelcome.msg # You have a security banner in /etc/issue.net, right?
chown root:root /home/user/.ftpwelcome.msg
chmod 444 /home/user/.ftpwelcome.msg # Keep the user from tampering with the message or
chattr +i /home/user/.ftpwelcome.msg # disabling it.
for file in .rhosts .shosts .netrc .forward ; do # Script the creation and lockdown
  touch $file     # of some sensitive files.
  chown root:root $file
  chmod 0 $file
  chattr +i $file
  done
rm .bash* .gtk*   # Since he'll never login, he'll never need shell files
```

Now test the server:

```
[user@otherhost user]$ ftp 192.168.1.20
Connected to 192.168.1.20.
220 FTP server ready.
User (192.168.1.20:(none)): luser
331 Password required for luser.
Password:
230-### WARNING ###
```

```
230-
230-This automated information system is for the exclusive use of
230-Systems Engineering personnel. Use of this system
230-without privilege or in excess of granted authority is forbidden, and
230-may be subject to civil and criminal penalties up to and including the
230-fullest extent permitted by law.
230-
230-Users accessing this system are subject to having their actions
230-monitored and recorded at any time. Use or access of this system in
230-any fashion constitutes expressed knowledge and acceptance of this
230-policy.
230-
230-### WARNING ###
230-
230 User luser logged in. Access restrictions apply.
ftp> pwd
257 "/" is current directory.
ftp> ls -la
200 PORT command successful.
150 Opening ASCII mode data connection for directory listing.
total 24
drwx—— 2 2501   2501   4096 Aug 18 22:39 .
drwx—— 2 2501   2501   4096 Aug 18 22:39 ..
——— 1 root  root    0 Aug 18 22:39 .forward
-r—r—r— 1 root  root   554 Aug 18 22:38 .ftpwelcome.msg
——— 1 root  root    0 Aug 18 22:39 .netrc
——— 1 root  root    0 Aug 18 22:39 .rhosts
——— 1 root  root    0 Aug 18 22:39 .shosts
226 Transfer complete.
ftp: 455 bytes received in 0.00Seconds 455000.00Kbytes/sec.
ftp> put foo.txt
200 PORT command successful.
150 Opening ASCII mode data connection for foo.txt.
226 Transfer complete.
```

```
ftp: 479 bytes sent in 0.00Seconds 479000.00Kbytes/sec.
ftp> del foo.txt
250 DELE command successful.
ftp> mkdir foo
257 "/foo" new directory created.
ftp> rmdir foo
250 RMD command successful.
ftp> cd /
250 CWD command successful.
ftp> ls -a
200 PORT command successful.
150 Opening ASCII mode data connection for directory listing.
.

..
.forward
.ftpwelcome.msg
.netrc
.rhosts
.shosts
226 Transfer complete.
ftp: 60 bytes received in 0.00Seconds 60000.00Kbytes/sec.
ftp> cd ../../../../../etc
550 ../../../../../etc: No such file or directory.
ftp> bye
221-You have transferred 466 bytes in 1 files.
221-Total traffic for this session was 2347 bytes in 1 transfers.
221-Thank you for using the FTP service on ftpserver.mydomain.com.
221 Goodbye.
```

3.3.1.2 Anonymous File Serving

To enable an anonymous FTP server, we only require a little further tweaking of the configuration file, and the careful creation of an FTP server root directory. Anonymous FTP servers should be handled like live snakes: treat them carefully, don't trust them fully, and keep them as far away from sensitive areas as possible! Thankfully, the combination of a good default ftpaccess file and the ease of configuring this latest WUFTPd means that anonymous FTP services can be configured with a minimum of heartburn.

First, we'll need to add some information to `/etc/ftpaccess`, <u>in addition</u> to the changes made above. Both sets of changes have been presented below, for simplicity's sake, but be careful to enter all of these changes to keep things nice and secure.

/etc/ftpaccess

- Don't allow system accounts to login over FTP.
  ```
  deny-uid %-99 %65534-
  deny-gid %-99 %65534-
  ```
- Chroot all users by default
  ```
  guestuser *
  ```
- List any users you wish to grant "real" privileges to (i.e. that should not be chrooted) here
  ```
  realuser <ftp administrators, etc.>
  ```
- We don't need an explicit chroot group: all users will be chrooted!
  ```
  # guestgroup ftpchroot
  ```
- Set your email address
  ```
  email ftpadmin@ftpserver.mydomain.com
  ```
- Permit only 2 failed logins before terminating the session
  ```
  loginfails 2
  ```
- Set the welcome message to something we can control and eliminate from directory listings
  ```
  message /.ftpwelcome.msg          login
  ```
- Do not allow on-the-fly tarring and compressing
  ```
  compress   no    all
  tar        no    all
  ```
- Prevent certain actions by anonymous and/or guest users. Explicitly list permissions for everyone.
  ```
  chmod       no    guest,anonymous
  delete      no    anonymous
  overwrite   no    anonymous
  rename      no    anonymous
  umask       no    real,guest,anonymous
  delete      yes   real,guest
  overwrite   yes   real,guest
  rename      yes   real,guest
  ```
- Log commands and transfers to and from the server (this will not log passwords unless the user types one as a command by mistake).
  ```
  log commands real,anonymous,guest
  ```

```
log transfers anonymous,guest,real inbound,outbound
```
- Mark certain files as non-retrievable
```
noretrieve .notar
noretrieve .ftpwelcome.msg
```
- Set up permissions for anonymous users within their file structure. Anonymous users may not upload files anywhere except specifically-configured areas.
```
upload /usr/local/ftp * no
```
- Anonymous users may upload files to their incoming directory, but the files will be immediately owned by a different user and group on the server and changed to read-only for members of that group. This will prevent the anonymous users from listing the contents of the incoming directory, preventing them from turning it into a wAreZ storehouse. They won't be able to retrieve anything from that directory either, and can't create subdirectories.

  upload /usr/local/ftp/incoming yes ftpusers ftpusers 0040 nodirs
- Set a secure path filter to weed out evil files
```
path-filter guest,anonymous /etc/pathmsg ^[-A-Za-z0-9_\.]*$ ^\. ^-
```
- Shorten the greeting string so as not to provide the server version
```
greeting terse
```
- Use secure default umasks for everyone
```
defumask 0377
defumask 0177 real
defumask 0133 guest
```

Next, we'll need to create the anonymous file directory. Mercifully, we no longer have to create binary or library directories, just file storage areas. Be careful with the permissions in this area! First, we'll need a user and group with no privileges: they'll wind up owning uploaded files, which "real" users on the system (who have been added to that group) can login through SSH and copy to other areas of the server to retrieve:

```
useradd -d /usr/local/ftp -s /dev/null ftpusers
passwd -l ftpusers
```

Now we can create the storage tree in /usr/local/ftp:

```
mkdir /usr/local/ftp
cd /usr/local/ftp
mkdir incoming
```

```
mkdir pub
chmod 755 pub
chown ftp:ftpusers incoming          # Note the "ftp" user here: that's so the
                                     anonymous user can write to this directory.

chmod 0370 incoming                  # Grant write and execute privileges for
                                     storage, but no reads

chown root:root pub                  # /pub will be a read-only file retrieval area
cp /etc/issue.net ./.ftpwelcome.msg  # You have a security banner in /etc/issue.net,
                                     right?

chown root:root ./.ftpwelcome.msg
chmod 444 ./.ftpwelcome.msg          # Keep the user from tampering with the
                                     message or disabling it.

chattr +i ./.ftpwelcome.msg
for file in .rhosts .shosts .netrc .forward ; do   # Script the creation and lockdown
    touch $file                      # of some sensitive files.
    chown root:root $file
    chmod 0 $file
    chattr +i $file
    done
rm .bash* .gtk*                      # Since he'll never login, he'll never need
                                     shell files
```

Finally, change the home directory for the `ftp` user in `/etc/passwd` to the new FTP server directory at `/usr/local/ftp`:

```
ftp:x:14:50:FTP User:/var/ftp:/sbin/nologin
```

becomes

```
ftp:x:14:50:FTP User:/usr/local/ftp:/sbin/nologin
```

Now you can test the server:

```
[user@other user]# ftp 192.168.1.20
Connected to 192.168.1.20 (192.168.1.20).
```

```
220 FTP server ready.
Name (192.168.1.20:user): anonymous
331 Guest login ok, send your complete e-mail address as password.
Password:
230-### WARNING ###
230-
230-This automated information system is for the exclusive use of
230-Systems Engineering personnel. Use of this system
230-without privilege or in excess of granted authority is forbidden, and
230-may be subject to civil and criminal penalties up to and including the
230-fullest extent permitted by law.
230-
230-Users accessing this system are subject to having their actions
230-monitored and recorded at any time. Use or access of this system in
230-any fashion constitutes expressed knowledge and acceptance of this
230-policy.
230-
230-### WARNING ###
230-
230 Guest login ok, access restrictions apply.
Remote system type is UNIX.
Using binary mode to transfer files.
ftp> ls
227 Entering Passive Mode (10,1,1,47,87,244)
150 Opening ASCII mode data connection for directory listing.
total 16
d-wxrwx— 2 14   2500    4096 Aug 18 22:07 incoming
drwxr-xr-x 2 root  root    4096 Aug 18 22:02 pub
226 Transfer complete.
ftp> mkdir asdf
550 asdf: Permission denied on server. (Upload dirs)
ftp> cd pub
250 CWD command successful.
ftp> mkdir asdf
```

```
550 asdf: Permission denied on server. (Upload dirs)
ftp> ls
227 Entering Passive Mode (10,1,1,47,179,115)
150 Opening ASCII mode data connection for directory listing.
total 8
-rw-r—r— 1 root   root    3859 Aug 18 22:02 osshChroot-3.4.diff
226 Transfer complete.
ftp> get osshChroot-3.4.diff
local: osshChroot-3.4.diff remote: osshChroot-3.4.diff
227 Entering Passive Mode (10,1,1,47,236,173)
150 Opening BINARY mode data connection for osshChroot-3.4.diff (3859 bytes).
226 Transfer complete.
3859 bytes received in 0.000342 secs (1.1e+04 Kbytes/sec)
ftp> del osshChroot-3.4.diff
553 osshChroot-3.4.diff: Permission denied on server. (Delete)
ftp> cd ../incoming
250 CWD command successful.
ftp> ls
227 Entering Passive Mode (10,1,1,47,205,141)
150 Opening ASCII mode data connection for directory listing.
total 0
226 Transfer complete.
ftp> put osshChroot-3.4.diff
local: osshChroot-3.4.diff remote: osshChroot-3.4.diff
227 Entering Passive Mode (10,1,1,47,242,244)
150 Opening BINARY mode data connection for osshChroot-3.4.diff.
226 Transfer complete.
3859 bytes sent in 0.0105 secs (3.6e+02 Kbytes/sec)
ftp> ls
227 Entering Passive Mode (10,1,1,47,9,59)
150 Opening ASCII mode data connection for directory listing.
total 0
226 Transfer complete.
ftp> ls -a
```

```
227 Entering Passive Mode (10,1,1,47,155,95)
150 Opening ASCII mode data connection for directory listing.
total 0
226 Transfer complete.
ftp> ls -la
227 Entering Passive Mode (10,1,1,47,48,107)
150 Opening ASCII mode data connection for directory listing.
total 0
226 Transfer complete.
ftp> get osshChroot-3.4.diff
local: osshChroot-3.4.diff remote: osshChroot-3.4.diff
227 Entering Passive Mode (10,1,1,47,67,94)
550 /incoming/osshChroot-3.4.diff is marked unretrievable
ftp> mkdir asdf
550 asdf: Permission denied on server. (Upload dirs)
ftp> exit
221-You have transferred 7718 bytes in 2 files.
221-Total traffic for this session was 10482 bytes in 2 transfers.
221-Thank you for using the FTP service on ftpserver.mydomain.com.
221 Goodbye.
[user@other user]#
```

3.3.2 NFS Security

The words "NFS" and "security" are not usually used in the same sentence together, unless it's a discussion of the lack of the latter in the former. There are times, however, when NFS is the simplest answer to solving a problem: sharing filesystems between multiple servers is never a simple problem, and NFS is sometimes the path of least resistance. The following section should assist administrators in securing this service as much as possible without vast complication.

We'll discuss two possible configurations: one featuring a transient filesystem that is only mounted when needed, and one featuring a more permanent filesystem mount, such as a shared set of home directories or system library or binary directories for thin clients.

3.3.2.1 NFS Server Security

Before attempting any sort of file sharing from an NFS server, it is a good idea to take some basic steps to secure the server's configuration. One major problem with NFS is its reliance on RPC-based services: rather than being assigned to a fixed port, RPC services are assigned a port randomly (or semi-randomly, or in some cases, not randomly at all) when they are initiated, by the RPC portmapper daemon. Clients wishing to connect to those services will first contact the portmapper daemon to inquire to which port the needed service has been assigned. Among other things, this plays havoc with firewalls, which rely on services being assigned a particular port time and again, which can make firewalling NFS services very difficult.

Fortunately, Red Hat's NFS implementation reduces this headache considerably through the use of some thoughtful configuration options: with the following quick changes, we can make NFS as firewall-friendly as possible.

3.3.2.1.1 Portmapper

First, we need to configure the portmapper daemon. It is always assigned the same port (TCP and UDP 111), so we don't need to worry about fixing that, but we do need to restrict access to it. Since this will be the gateway to the NFS services on the server, we need to carefully control to whom we grant access. By default, the portmapper daemon on Red Hat Linux comes compiled with support for Wietse Venema's TCP wrappers, which allows us to control access to it using a pair of configuration files. In `/etc/hosts.deny`, we'll first set a default-deny policy for the portmapper:

```
/etc/hosts.deny
portmap: ALL
```

Now we'll configure `/etc/hosts.allow` to permit access to the portmapper from trusted internal machines. Add IP addresses into this file to permit NFS clients access to the portmapper, being careful to list specific IPs rather than subnets, where possible. Below, we've granted access only to the NFS client at IP address 10.1.2.3.

```
/etc/hosts.allow
portmap: 10.1.2.3
```

3.3.2.1.2 mountd

The mount daemon (mountd) actually implements NFS mount requests: when a client wishes to mount a filesystem over NFS, it sends a MOUNT request to mountd to initiate the process, who verifies the request against the list of exported filesystems and returns a filehandle of the filesystem if the request is approved.

Mountd is an RPC service, so the first thing to do is to lock in the port to which it will be assigned. Anticipating this desire, Red Hat has configured a simple way to do this by adding the information to a configuration file rather than having to edit the startup file for this service by hand. First, choose a port for the mount daemon: it can be any port number higher than 1024, with the default choice being 2050 most of the time. Once you've selected your port, edit `/etc/sysconfig/network` as follows (we've used 2050 as an example):

```
/etc/sysconfig/network
MOUNTD_PORT=2050
```

On Red Hat Linux, mountd has also been compiled with support for TCP wrappers, so this service can be granted additional security by permitting access only from selected clients. This prevents an NFS problem in which clients could bypass restrictions on the portmapper and mount a filesystem by sending the request directly to mountd if they could figure out on what port mountd was running. To implement this, edit `/etc/hosts.deny` and `/etc/hosts.allow` again and add to the bottom the following lines (as an example, we've again granted access only to the NFS client at IP address 10.1.2.3):

```
/etc/hosts.deny
mountd: ALL
/etc/hosts.allow
mountd: 10.1.2.3
```

3.3.2.1.3 nfsd

The NFS daemon (nfsd) is a sort of go-between, shuttling information back and forth between the userland space and the kernel module (nfsd.o) actually implementing NFS under Linux. Like mountd, nfsd is an RPC service, so it has no fixed port, and unlike mountd, it has not been compiled with support for TCP wrappers nor does it have a convenient shortcut in the system configuration files for pre-selecting a port. However, we can pre-select the port on it by editing the startup script (`/etc/init.d/nfs`) by hand and adding the following information:

```
/etc/init.d/nfs
```

Find this block:

```
echo -n $"Starting NFS daemon: "
daemon rpc.nfsd $RPCNFSDCOUNT
```

And change it to read thus (using 2049 as our pre-selected port for nfsd):

```
echo -n $"Starting NFS daemon: "
daemon rpc.nfsd -p 2049 $RPCNFSDCOUNT
```

3.3.2.1.4 Rquotad

The remote quota daemon (`rquotad`) is responsible for answering clients' queries about user quotas for exported NFS filesystems. That is, when a client attempts to write to an NFS filesystem, it will first inquire of the quota daemon (if the server has quotas active for that filesystem) whether the client has sufficient quota to issue the write. Rquotad will then check the local quotas for that user and return that information to the client. Unfortunately, in addition to lacking TCP wrappers support, rquotad cannot be fixed to a specific port. If you wish to tie user quotas to NFS, you will need to plan for this, since rquotad cannot be further secured.

On the other hand, if you are not using quotas, there is no reason to run rquotad, and you can deactivate it without having an impact on your NFS filesystems. To do so, edit the NFS startup script (`/etc/init.d/nfs`):

```
/etc/init.d/nfs
```

Comment out the following blocks in this file to deactivate rquotad:

```
if [ -x /usr/sbin/rpc.rquotad ] ; then
 echo -n $"Starting NFS quotas: "
 daemon rpc.rquotad
 echo
fi

if [ -x /usr/sbin/rpc.rquotad ] ; then
 echo -n $"Stopping NFS quotas: "
 killproc rpc.rquotad
 echo
fi

if [ -x /usr/sbin/rpc.rquotad ] ; then
 status rpc.rquotad
fi
```

You'll notice that all of these blocks check to see if `rpc.rquotad` is executable (using the `-x` flag) before running these commands. One possible way of deactivating rquotad is to remove the executable bits from it using `chmod` (`chmod a-x /usr/sbin/rpc.rquotad` would work). While this would deactivate it, an RPM update to quota RPM (or a well-meaning administrator!) would likely restore those executable privileges, thus inadvertently reactivating the daemon. If you've really decided not to use quotas over NFS, commenting those blocks will help guarantee that the service stays deactivated until you choose to activate it. Obviously, if the service is not needed, you should uninstall it to keep it from being a liability to the system in the future: a quick 'rpm -e quota' will accomplish this.

3.3.2.2 NFS Client Security
Securing the client is relatively simple: it will only require the portmapper. The mount command will handle the necessary NFS module

activations when called upon to mount a filesystem over NFS. Since the client will be running the portmapper, however, this should be secured in the same manner as the server's, restricting inbound connections to only those necessary.

3.3.2.2.1 Example I: Transient Filesystem

In this example, we'll present a sample configuration for a secured NFS mount between a client and server which would be mounted manually by administrators. This would include shared directories that contain system patches, for example, so that a central patch repository could be remotely mounted to patch servers and then unmounted when not needed. Since the directory containing the patches will only be read by the client and should not be altered, we can export this filesystem read-only. We can also export the filesystem using "squashing", an option that maps UIDs and GIDs on the client to corresponding UIDs and GIDs on the server. Commonly, this is done to the root account, so that the remote client's root account is not automatically granted root-level privileges to the filesystems on the server. In this case, however, we only need the right to read the patches, so we'll export the filesystem with complete squashing: we'll create an unprivileged user on the server who can only read the patches, and map all remote UIDs to that user, reducing all of the client's privileges accordingly. NFS also allows us to export the filesystem to a specific client or group of clients: *never* export a filesystem to the world! We'll restrict access to the patches share to a local, internal subnet: 10.1.1.0/24, e.g.

Linux offers some convenient extra tweaks to NFS to tighten security a little: the "hide" feature, enabled by default, means that a filesystem mounted within a shared filesystem (such as having /usr and /usr/local on separate disk partitions) is not automatically shared: the server must share that secondary filesystem separately, and the client must mount it separately. In addition, the "secure" feature, also enabled by default, requires that NFS mount requests originate from a privileged port, helping to ensure that the user making the remote mount request is root or has root privileges. This isn't a foolproof determinant, but every little bit helps.

On the Server

1. Create the patch directory
   ```
   mkdir /local/patches
   ```
2. Create the unprivileged user and group
   ```
   groupadd -g 1500 patches
   useradd -u 1500 -g patches -d /local/patches -s /dev/null patches
   ```
3. Edit /etc/exports to configure the share
   ```
   /etc/exports
   /local/patches   10.1.1.0/24(ro,secure,hide,all_squash,anonuid=1500,anongid=1500)
   ```
4. Ensure that the NFS services are running on the server
   ```
   /etc/init.d/portmap start
   /etc/init.d/nfs start
   /etc/init.d/nfslock start
   ```

5. Export all configured filesystem shares (-a), using verbose output (-v)

```
/usr/sbin/exportfs -va
```

6. Copy patches into `/local/patches`

On the Client

1. Ensure the portmapper is running

```
/etc/init.d/portmap start
```

2. Create the mount point

```
mkdir /nfsmount/patches
```

3. Mount the remote filesystem from the server at 10.1.1.50

```
/bin/mount -t nfs 10.1.1.50:/local/patches /nfsmount/patches
```

3.3.2.2.2 Example II: At-Boot Filesystem

The example being explored here is a filesystem that would be mounted at boot off of a central fileserver. Frequently, this is done with user home directories. Since the users will need individual access to their directories, we cannot employ complete squashing as we did in the previous example. Instead, we'll be sure to use root squashing. In order to do this, you must be careful to synchronize UIDs between the clients and the server. Since access is granted by numerical UID and not by username, a user with a different UID on the client and the server would not have access rights to her own directory, and might (even worse) have complete access to someone else's entirely!

On the Server

1. Create the users for whom you'll want to grant access, and synchronize their UIDs with the client. If the users will not ever login to the NFS server directly, they can be granted user accounts with null shells (/dev/null or /bin/false or the like), since that account information will then only be used for mapping NFS privileges. We can at least restrict the access to this filesystem to the local LAN (as is almost always a good idea for security), and we can employ root squashing to prevent root-level breaches.

2. Edit `/etc/exports` to configure the share

```
/etc/exports
/home   10.1.1.0/24(rw,secure,hide,root_squash)
```

3. Ensure that the NFS services are running on the server

```
/etc/init.d/portmap start
/etc/init.d/nfs start
/etc/init.d/nfslock start
```

4. Export all configured filesystem shares (-a), using verbose output (-v)

```
/usr/sbin/exportfs -va
```

On the Client

One extra piece of security checking to be performed: the client should mount the filesystem as an untrusted volume. This means mounting it without SUID files (nosuid), without devices (nodev) and preferably without executables, to prevent the server from being granted additional privileges on the client. The first two options are particularly important: without them, an attacker with access to the NFS server could insert a SUID shell or compromised device into the shared filesystem and be automatically granted privileges on the other filesystems. Although we've enabled root squashing, remember that there is no squashing for users such as bin or daemon, which are potentially just as dangerous to the client as root access!

1. Ensure the portmapper is running

```
/etc/init.d/portmap start
```

2. Test connectivity by mounting the remote filesystem from the server at 10.1.1.50

```
/bin/mount -t nfs 10.1.1.50:/home /home
```

3. Configure /etc/fstab to mount the filesystem automatically

```
/etc/fstab:
```

```
10.1.1.50:/home  /home  nfs  nosuid,nodev,noexec 0 0
```

3.3.3 SAMBA Security (http://www.samba.org/)

As much as many Unix administrators revile it, Microsoft's Windows family of operating systems are a fact of modern life at most companies. Fortunately, the interoperability of Unix and Windows hosts is alive and well, thanks both to considerable hard work from open standards bodies such as the IETF, and thanks to programs like Samba. Samba, in the words of its creators, "is an Open Source/Free Software suite that provides seamless file and print services to SMB/CIFS clients." (http://us2.samba.org/samba/samba.html).

SMB/CIFS is a standard developed by Microsoft to offer shared file and print services; thanks to the hard work of the Samba development team, Unix hosts can join in the CIFS fun as clients and as servers, even to the point of masquerading as Windows NT Domain Servers for an entire network of Windows hosts, none of whom will notice the difference.

This section eschews a general configuration discussion of Samba, and focuses on securing Samba on Red Hat Linux 7.3, using the supplied Red Hat packages. We will configure Samba as a server to share files and printers securely, and as a client.

3.3.3.1 SAMBA Server

Configuring Samba as a server is fairly simple, once you have the packages for Samba installed. First, decide what filesystems and/or printers you will share to other hosts. Then follow these instructions. For this example, we'll configure a server that will share out user home directories and its printers for its local users. The server will live at IP 192.168.1.20, and will permit IPs in the 192.168.1 network to mount its shares. To increase the security of this configuration, the server will not be part of a domain, but will instead use a local password file for users, who will not be granted command-line access to the server.

1. Install the Samba packages
```
rpm -ivh samba-2.2.3a-6.i386.rpm
rpm -ivh samba-common-2.2.3a-6.i386.rpm
```

2. You'll need to assemble some information:
   - Your NT domain name or workgroup name:
   - List of hosts or networks to grant access to this server's shares:
   - IP of NT domain server, if applicable:

3. Edit the main Samba configuration file, `/etc/samba/smb.conf` (changes excerpted and highlighted in **bold,** with comments in *italics*):

/etc/samba/smb.conf

\# workgroup = NT-Domain-Name or Workgroup-Name

 # Set this field to your NT domain name or the name of your Windows Workgroup

workgroup = Mygroup

\# Server string is the equivalent of the NT Description field

 # Change this string to something innocuous, per your organization's standards.

 # This information will show up in the "Network Neighborhood" browser for users on the

 # network.

server string = Home directory server

 # Set the list of hosts allowed to connect to this one for services

 # Be sure to use only IP addresses in this list: hostnames can be spoofed.

 # The following are all valid IPs for this list:

 # 192.168.1. would choose all IPs starting with 192.168.1.

 # 127. would choose anything on the loopback network (e.g. 127.0.0.1)

 # 192.168.1.47 would choose only this host

hosts allow = 192.168.1.

 # Server security level:
 # This will set the method by which Samba authenticates users for shares. Do NOT set this
 # to "share", as this can allow remote clients to mount shares by only sending a username
 # for access.
 # Set this to "user" (as is the default) if you are a standalone server, not part of an NT
 # domain.
 # If this machine is part of an NT domain, use smbpasswd to add it to the domain, and then
 # set this value to "domain" to authenticate against the domain server.
```
security = user
```

 # Password Level should be set to zero: unless you're using Windows 95 or 98, current Windows
 # versions can handle properly encoding password strings. Win95, Win98, and Windows for
 # Workgroups had a habit of sending passwords in all-upper-case letters, which would cause
 # password checks to fail unless you set this parameter to have the server try setting
 # various letters in the password to lower-case. A similar thing happens with the username
 # and older DOS-based clients.
```
password level = 0
username level = 0
```

 # Enable password encryption, to be stored in the smbpasswd file. Fortunately, Red Hat uses
 # the right behavior by default.
```
encrypt passwords = yes
smb passwd file = /etc/samba/smbpasswd
```

 # Commenting the following lines prevents synchronization of Unix and SMB passwords, which
 # in this case is what we want, to keep the two databases separate. We're going to lock
 # the local user accounts and only grant Samba access.
```
  unix password sync = no
# passwd program = /usr/bin/passwd %u
# passwd chat = *New*password [etc.]
  pam password change = no
```

 # Instruct Samba to map NT users to local Unix accounts using this file
username map = /etc/samba/smbusers

 # Do not have Samba act as a domain logon server for Windows 95 workstations
domain logons = no

 # Now we define the shares
 # Here are the home directories
```
[homes]
   comment = Home Directories
```
 # Do not list these shares without authentication, e.g. in "Network Neighborhood"
```
   browseable = no
   writable = yes
```
 # User accounts are normally valid...
```
   valid users = %S
```
 # ...unless they appear in this list. Note the use of "@wheel" to designate anyone
 # in the "wheel" group.
```
   invalid users = root bin daemon adm lp sync halt shutdown mail news uucp operator \
         games gopher ftp nobody vcsa mailnull ntp rpc xfs gdm rpcuser nfsnobody nscd pcap @wheel
```
 # Set the default umask
create mode = 644
 # Set the default permissions mode for shared directories
directory mode = 755

```
# Here are the printer shares
[printers]
   comment = Shared Printers
   path = /var/spool/samba
```
 # Do not list printer shares without authentication, e.g. in "Network Neighborhood"
```
   browseable = no
```
 # Users must be authenticated to use these printers
```
   guest ok = no
```
 # Users may not remove or disable these printers
```
   writable = no
   printable = yes
```

4. Create a user on the Samba server

a. First, we'll create the user, with a locked shell

```
useradd -u 1500 -d /home/user -s /dev/null -m user
```

b. Next we can lock the user's local password, and set the Samba password, which will be stored in Samba's separate password database, /etc/samba/smbpasswd

```
passwd -l user
smbpasswd -a user
[Enter a password for this user to authenticate for Samba shares]
```

5. Start up the Samba services, and you should be able to map a drive as that user from a Windows machine on the network.

```
/etc/init.d/smb start
```

Samba Client

Next, we'll mount a share from a Windows server on the same network, using smbmount, then configure it to mount at boot.

1. Check that you can mount the share from the command line. For our example, the server will be named saturn, at IP 192.168.1.20, with a client named mercury at IP 192.168.1.50. We'll mount a shared directory to a local directory named /local/samba on mercury. To ease our configuration a little, we'll add saturn to the hosts file on mercury, so we can locate it by name quickly.

```
[root@mercury root]# echo "192.168.1.20<tab>saturn" >> /etc/hosts
[root@mercury root]# echo >> /etc/hosts
[root@mercury root]# mount -t smbfs -o username=user,workgroup=MYGROUP \
//saturn/shared /local/samba
Password: <Enter password>
[root@mercury root]# ls /local/samba
somefiles somemorefiles someotherfiles
[root@mercury root]# umount /local/samba
```

2. Next, we'll secure the mount as much as we can: we'll create an unprivileged user and corresponding group to own the files in the directory, and set the mount to be group-accessible only. Any users who need access to these files should be added to the group.

```
useradd -u 5000 -d /local/samba -s /dev/null smbowner
passwd -l smbowner
```

3. Unfortunately, since the mount point requires authentication, there is no way for the client to create the mount without entering a password of some kind. Since /etc/fstab needs to be world-readable, we'll instead store the credentials for this mount in a file within root's home directory, and make them readable only by root. You can also opt to mark the mount point as not automatically mounted at boot time (`noauto`), and mount it by hand when you reboot, entering the password at the console or over a secure login session. This is more secure, but means that unattended reboots will make the filesystem vanish until someone connects to the server and manually mounts it.

```
[root@client root]# cat >> /root/.smbmount
    username = NTUser          # Make these values very secure and don't make them the same as
    password = NTPassword # any other credentials for any other server!
    [ Press <Ctrl>-D ]
[root@client root]# chmod 400 /root/.smbmount
[root@client root]# chown root /root/.smbmount
[root@client root]# chattr +i /root/.smbmount
```

4. Edit /etc/fstab and set up the mount options

```
/etc/fstab
    [...]
    # The following should be all on one line
    //saturn/shared /local/samba    smbfs credentials=/root/.smbmount,workgroup=MYGROUP \
    uid=smbowner,gid=smbowner 0 0
```

5. In order for your filesystem to mount automatically at boot, you either have to hack /etc/rc.d/rc.sysinit or else run the `netfs` service on your machine, which automatically mounts any network-based filesystems configured in /etc/fstab. Without that service, Samba filesystems will not be mounted automatically. To turn it on, run this command:

```
/sbin/chkconfig —level 2345 netfs on
```

3.3.4 SCP and SFTP

The need for remote file-transfer and command-line control sessions is of paramount importance to Unix administrators. For many years, however, only protocols such as FTP, Telnet and RSH were available. These protocols transmitted not only the data of the session but the authentication information as well in cleartext over the network. The advent of the Secure Shell (ssh) protocol introduced a much-welcomed answer to this problem, providing complete encryption of both command-line and data transfer sessions using strong encryption algorithms. Particularly welcome has been the recent development of OpenSSH, a spinoff of the OpenBSD project, which has helped bring this protocol into wider use with its open-source implementation that compiles on any number of different Unix platforms. As a result, most Linux distributions now ship with OpenSSH pre-installed.

While configuration of SSH for command sessions is covered in another section of this text, one feature that is sometimes overlooked is its file-transfer capabilities, intended to replace rcp and ftp at one blow. The `scp` and `sftp` commands do an excellent job of replacing their non-encrypted counterparts, emulating the command-line switches and options so well that in most cases, `scp` in particular can simply be used as a drop-in replacement for `rcp`. In this section, we'll configure an SSH server such that file transfers using `sftp` are as secure as possible, including the use of chroot to jail the users' file-transfer sessions, by patching the SSH source code. Unfortunately, the patch currently does not work for scp, but chrooted and non-chrooted users can exist side-by-side.

Red Hat, even with the most current patches, does not always offer the latest SSH build, so it will be necessary to get the portable distribution of OpenSSH from the OpenSSH team (http://www.openssh.com). You can fetch the portable version in a binary RPM, source RPM, or gzipped source tarball; since the chroot will require modifications to the code, we'll need one of the two latter options.

If you're not interested in implementing the chroot feature, you can skip ahead: you'll need the configuration files for SSH featured at the end of this section and you'll be set.

3.3.4.1 Chrooting SFTP

1. Fetch and unpack the sources

Table 3-4. Fetching and Unpacking Sources

Using Source Tarball	Using Source RPM
cd /usr/src	cd /usr/src
tar zxvf /usr/src/openssh-3.4p1.tar.gz	rpm -ivh /usr/src/openssh-3.4p1-1.src.rpm
cd /usr/src/openssh-3.4p1	cp /usr/src/osshChroot-3.4.diff /usr/src/redhat/SOURCES
patch -p1 < /usr/src/osshChroot-3.4.diff	cd /usr/src/redhat/SPECS
	add lines to /usr/src/redhat/SPECS/openssh.spec (See end of section for modifications to spec file)

2. Configure, build and install the package

Table 3-5. Configuring, Building, and Installing Packages

Using Source Tarball	Using Source RPM
./configure \ —prefix=/usr\ —with-tcp-wrappers \ —with-rsh=/bin/rsh \ —with-default-path=/usr/local/bin:/usr/bin:/bin \ —with-superuser-path=\ /usr/local/sbin:/usr/local/bin:/sbin:/bin:/usr/sbin:/usr/bin \ —with-privsep-path=/var/empty/sshd \ —with-ipv4-default \ —with-pam \ —with-md5-passwords	rpm -bb /usr/src/redhat/SPECS/openssh.spec
make	cd /usr/src/redhat/RPMS/i386
make install	[If you already have Red Hat's SSH installed] rpm -Fvh /usr/src/redhat/RPMS/i386/openssh*.rpm [If this is a fresh install of SSH] cd /usr/src/redhat/RPMS/i386 rpm -ivh ./openssh-3.4p1-1.i386.rpm rpm -ivh ./openssh-clients-3.4p1-1.i386.rpm rpm -ivh ./openssh-server-3.4p1-1.i386.rpm

3. Create the chroot directory

```
/bin/mkdir /usr/local/chroot
cd /usr/local/chroot
/bin/mkdir -p bin dev/pts lib/i686 home usr/bin usr/libexec/openssh usr/lib etc var/log
for prog in bash cp ls mkdir mv rm rmdir ; do
  /bin/cp -p /bin/$prog /usr/local/chroot/bin
  done
```

```
for file in ld-linux.so.2 libcrypto.so.2 libdl.so.2 libnsl.so.1 libtermcap.so.2 libutil.so.1 ; do
  /bin/cp -p /lib/$file /usr/local/chroot/lib
  done
/bin/cp -p /lib/i686/libc.so.6 /usr/local/chroot/lib/i686/libc.so.6
/bin/cp -p /usr/lib/libz.so.1 /usr/local/chroot/lib/libz.so.1
cd /usr/local/chroot/dev
/bin/mknod null c 1 3
/bin/mknod tty c 5 0
/bin/mknod zero c 1 5
/bin/mknod pts/0 c 136 0
/bin/mknod pts/1 c 136 1
/bin/chmod 650 pts/*
/bin/chmod 666 tty null zero
/bin/touch /usr/local/chroot/etc/passwd
```

4. Test the chroot

To ensure the chroot is working properly, we'll chroot a shell as root. Since sftp uses chroot behind the scenes to perform its actions, we need to make sure that a chrooted shell will have all of the libraries it needs.

```
[root@host root]# /usr/sbin/chroot /usr/local/chroot /bin/bash
bash-2.05a# ls
bin dev etc home lib usr var
bash-2.05a# exit
[root@host root]#
```

5. Create the chrooted user account

We will create a single user account to test the chroot: note that the home directory for this user will contain "/ . /" as a trigger to the SSH daemon to activate the chroot when this user logs in. This means that users without that trigger can login normally and see the whole filesystem (and will be able to use scp), whereas the chrooted users will use sftp and will be limited to only their own directories.

```
/usr/sbin/useradd -d /usr/local/chroot/./home/chuser -s /bin/bash -m chuser
/bin/grep chuser /etc/passwd >> /usr/local/chroot/etc/passwd
```

```
/bin/chmod 444 /usr/local/chroot/etc/passwd
/usr/bin/chattr +i /usr/local/chroot/etc/passwd
```

6. Run the daemon and test the chroot by transferring a file

```
[root@host root]# /usr/sbin/sshd -D
(From another host)
[root@other root]# sftp chuser@ssh-host
chuser@ssh-host's password: <Enter password>
sftp> ls
drwx—— 2 2000 2000 4096 Aug 15 23:07 .
drwxr-xr-x 3 0 0 4096 Aug 15 22:59 ..
-rw—— 1 2000 2000 68 Aug 15 22:52 .bash_history
-rw-r—r— 1 2000 2000 24 Aug 15 22:52 .bash_logout
-rw-r—r— 1 2000 2000 191 Aug 15 22:52 .bash_profile
-rw-r—r— 1 2000 2000 124 Aug 15 22:52 .bashrc
sftp> pwd
Remote working directory: /home/chuser
sftp> put foo
Uploading foo to /home/chuser/foo
sftp> ls
drwx—— 2 2000 2000 4096 Aug 15 23:07 .
drwxr-xr-x 3 0 0 4096 Aug 15 22:59 ..
-rw-r—r— 1 2000 2000 17371 Aug 15 23:19 foo
sftp> quit
[root@other root]#
```

[START HERE if you're NOT using the chroot patch for sftp]

7. Secure the daemon's configuration

On the server, modify /etc/ssh/sshd_config to match the version at the end of this section.
On all clients, modify /etc/ssh/ssh_config to match the version at the end of this section.
Create /etc/issue.net with a suitable warning banner; one is provided in the example section.

8. Create keypairs

File transfers can be automated (as one might like to do for log rotation and storage or automated backup routines) using RSA or DSA keypairs. To do this, follow these instructions to create your keypairs and transmit them to the server (we'll use a DSA keypair for this example).

On the client:

```
[user@host user]$ ssh-keygen -t dsa
Generating public/private dsa key pair.
Enter file in which to save the key (/home/user/.ssh/id_dsa): <Press Enter>
Enter passphrase (empty for no passphrase): <Enter a passphrase>
Enter same passphrase again: <Confirm your passphrase>
Your identification has been saved in /home/user/.ssh/id_dsa.
Your public key has been saved in /home/user/.ssh/id_dsa.pub.
The key fingerprint is:
7b:ab:75:32:9e:b6:6c:4b:29:dc:2a:2b:8c:2f:4e:37 user@host
[user@host user]$ ls -l ~/.ssh
-rw——— 1 user user 526 Aug 15 01:21 id_dsa
-rw-r—r— 1 user user 330 Aug 15 01:21 id_dsa.pub
[user@host user]$ cd ~/.ssh
[user@host user]$ sftp user@sftp-server
user@sftp-server's password: <Enter password>
sftp> put id_dsa.pub
Uploading id_dsa.pub to /home/user
sftp> exit
```

On the server:

```
[ Login as user on the SFTP server, either through SSH with a password or on the console ]
[user@host user]$ mkdir ~/.ssh
[user@host user]$ chmod 700 ~/.ssh
[user@host user]$ cd ~/.ssh
[user@host .ssh]$ mv ../id_dsa.pub ./authorized_keys2
```

```
[user@host .ssh]$ chmod 600 authorized_keys2
```

That should do it! If you entered a passphrase to encrypt the DSA keypair, you'll have to enter it on the client when connecting to the remote host (which is more secure, since the passphrase is never transmitted over the wire). For automated connections, you can create a keypair with a blank password by hitting `<CR>` when prompted for a passphrase to encrypt the keypair during the generation process. That will mean that anyone with the private half of that keypair (`id_dsa`) can login as that user, so be very careful to guard that file well!

Note: *The various "flavors" of SSH (the commercial version from ssh.com, OpenSSH, etc.) differ somewhat in their key formats, especially when exchanging keys between a Windows client and a Unix server. If you need to exchange keys between different flavors of ssh, one option is the ssh-keyinstall utility (http://www.stearns.org/ssh-keyinstall/).*

9. Add the daemon to the system startup scripts

If you've installed using the source RPM, a quick "`chkconfig —level 2345 sshd on`" will activate the SSH daemon; if not, use the SSH startup script in the section covering SSH daemon configuration elsewhere in this guide.

Note: Where files are modified, the unaltered text appears in a normal font, with the needed changes in **bold**.

/usr/src/redhat/SPECS/openssh.spec
[...]

 # Do we want to disable building of x11-askpass (1=yes 0=no)
%define no_x11_askpass **1**

 # Do we want to disable building of gnome-askpass (1=yes 0=no)
%define no_gnome_askpass **1**

[...]

 # Disable IPv6 (avoids DNS hangs on some glibc versions)
%define noip6 **1**

 # Do we want kerberos5 support (1=yes 0=no)
%define kerberos5 **0**

[...]

Source1: http://www.pobox.com/jmknoble/software/x11-ssh-askpass/x11-ssh-askpass-%[aversion].tar.gz
Patch0: http://chrootssh.sourceforge.net/patches/osshChroot-3.4.diff
License: BSD

[...]

%prep

%if ! %{no_x11_askpass}
%setup -q -a 1
%else
%setup -q
%endif

%patch -p 1

[...]

/etc/ssh/ssh_config

```
Host *
# Do not ask for port-forwarding by default
ForwardAgent no
# Do not ask for X11 forwarding by default
ForwardX11 no
# Do not ever use .rhosts files for authentication
RhostsAuthentication no
# Do not use .rhosts file for authentication, even with RSA keypairs
RhostsRSAAuthentication no
# Use keypairs for authentication, where available
RSAAuthentication yes
# Fall back to password authentication when necessary
```

```
PasswordAuthentication yes
```
By default, ask for passwords interactively
```
BatchMode no
```
Check that the host's IP matches the key it is presenting in the known_hosts file
```
CheckHostIP yes
```
Ask the user if she would like to add keys to the known_hosts file when an unknown key is presented
```
StrictHostKeyChecking ask
```
Use these files for RSA and DSA keypairs by default
```
IdentityFile ~/.ssh/identity
IdentityFile ~/.ssh/id_rsa
IdentityFile ~/.ssh/id_dsa
Port 22
```
Use only protocol 2 by default
```
Protocol 2
```
Try AES (Rijndael) encryption with a 192-bit key first
```
Cipher aes192-cbc
```
If that fails, try these ciphers in this order.
```
Ciphers aes192-cbc,aes256-cbc,aes128-cbc,blowfish-cbc,3des-cbc
```
Use this key to suspend the session to change settings
```
EscapeChar ~
```

/etc/ssh/sshd_config

Port 22
 # Use only version 2 of the protocol
Protocol 2
ListenAddress 0.0.0.0
HostKey /etc/ssh/ssh_host_rsa_key
HostKey /etc/ssh_ssh_host_dsa_key
SyslogFacility AUTH
LogLevel INFO
 # Offer the user 90 seconds to finish authenticating or time out the connection
LoginGraceTime 90
 # Do not permit root to login directly
PermitRootLogin no

```
StrictModes yes
RSAAuthentication yes
PubkeyAuthentication yes
AuthorizedKeysFile .ssh/authorized_keys
RhostsAuthentication no
IgnoreRhosts yes
RhostsRSAAuthentication no
HostbasedAuthentication no
IgnoreUserKnownHosts no
PasswordAuthentication yes
PermitEmptyPasswords no
# Do not use challenge-response-type authentication (unless you're using S/KEY, in which case you'll want to turn this on)
ChallengeResponseAuthentication no
KerberosAuthentication no
KerberosOrLocalPasswd yes
KerberosTicketCleanup yes
AFSTokenPassing no
KerberosTgtPassing no
PAMAuthenticationViaKbdInt yes
X11Forwarding no
X11DisplayOffset 10
X11UseLocalhost yes
PrintLastLog yes
KeepAlive yes
UseLogin no
UsePrivilegeSeparation yes
Compression yes
MaxStartups yes
# Print this banner prior to allowing the user to authenticate.
# Remember to put a system warning in this file!
Banner /etc/issue.net
VerifyReverseMapping no
Subsystem sftp /usr/libexec/openssh/sftp-server
```

3.4 DNS SECURITY - BIND

Securing DNS services can be a tricky and time-consuming task, requiring an administrator to spend a great deal of time planning and anticipating the organization's future growth and existing needs. The use of ISC's BIND DNS server (http://www.isc.org/products/BIND) has become an industry standard, marred by frequent discoveries of security problems either inherent in the server code or its design that have permitted attackers to compromise DNS servers, poison caches of DNS information and perform other such nefarious attacks on organizations. Proper design and deployment of a DNS server, especially one exposed in any way to the Internet, is therefore a paramount concern.

Fortunately, the recent spate of DNS attacks have caused those designing and maintaining the BIND code to design new safeguards for DNS information which, although somewhat cumbersome to establish, can help secure servers against attacks that might compromise or alter DNS information. We will explore below two common configurations for a DNS server: an internal caching DNS server, and a server which hosts DNS zones.

To maintain a high degree of security, both configurations will be confined to a "jail" on the server limiting their access: using the `chroot()` system call, the BIND server can be instructed to confine itself to a small area of the system as if that were the entire server. Any attacks that compromise the daemon will thus leave the attacker within the restricted area, unable to access any other portions of the server. In keeping with recent developments in BIND, we will deploy version 9 of the server: be sure, when you fetch the source code for this edition, that you are obtaining the latest stable release of the code possible, and always check with references such as BUGTRAQ to be sure there are no outstanding security breaches known for that version.

An exhaustive examination of all of the possible configurations and options for DNS would be well beyond the scope of this document: the user is directed to such works as Albitz and Liu's DNS and BIND (O'Reilly Publishing), now in its fourth edition, for a more encyclopedic reference to this protocol.

For all of the examples below, the following configuration has been used:

Internal network: 1.3.5.0 / 24
External network: 2.4.6.0 / 24
Domain: example.com
1.3.5.50 is the primary DNS server, with a secondary DNS server at 2.4.6.5. This network's ISP also offers a caching DNS server at 3.5.7.10.

3.4.1 Caching-only Nameserver

This nameserver will offer DNS service to a local network. Although it does not host any DNS domains (also called "zones"), it accepts queries from the local network and resolves them against a cache of recent requests. If it finds that it cannot answer the request from its own cache of information, it will (depending on its configuration) either forward the query upstream to the ISP's caching nameserver to see if *it* can answer the query, or can perform recursive queries out to the Internet on its own to discover the necessary information.

3.4.1.1 Unpack Sources and Compile Binaries

```
tar -zxvf bind-9.2.1.tar.gz
cd bind-9.2.1
```

Configure in OpenSSL support to enable transaction signing

```
./configure —with-openssl —with-randomdev=/dev/random
make
```

Here, we're going to use the DESTDIR option for installing the binaries directly into the chroot jail, which saves time.

```
mkdir /usr/local/bind
make install DESTDIR=/usr/local/bind
```

3.4.1.2 Set Up the Chroot Jail Environment

```
cd /usr/local/bind
```

Now we need to simulate the root environment, since this corner of the filesystem is all that the daemon will have access to while it is running.

```
mkdir -p dev etc named/local var/run
```

We need an unprivileged user account under which the server will run, with a separate and unique group. This permits the daemon to own files and directories to which it has to write, without overlapping those permissions with other areas of other filesystems.

```
useradd -s /dev/null -d /usr/local/bind dns
groupadd dns
```

The daemon will store several volatile files in /var/run in the jail, so it will need access to write to those.

```
chown -R dns:dns /usr/local/bind/var/run
```

While chrooted, the daemon will require access to system libraries and devices to answer requests. Since this miniature root filesystem is all that it will have access to while running, we need to replicate that information within the chroot. The libraries necessary were obtained by running `ldd` against the BIND binaries in `/usr/local/bind/sbin` to determine which libraries were compiled into them.

```
mknod /usr/local/bind/dev/null c 1 3
mknod /usr/local/bind/dev/random c 1 8
chmod 666 /usr/local/bind/dev/null /usr/local/bind/dev/random
cp /lib/libcrypto.so.2 /usr/local/bind/lib
cp /lib/libnsl.so.1 /usr/local/bind/lib
cp /lib/libc.so.6 /usr/local/bind/lib
cp /lib/libdl.so.2 /usr/local/bind/lib
cp /lib/ld-linux.so.2 /usr/local/bind/lib
cp /etc/localtime /usr/local/bind/etc
```

Here, we inform the syslog daemon that it may receive syslog information from an additional log socket: `/usr/local/bind/dev/log`, which resides within the chroot. This allows us to receive syslog messages from the chrooted daemon.

edit `/etc/sysconfig/syslog`:
```
SYSLOGD_OPTIONS="-m 0"
```

becomes
```
SYSLOGD_OPTIONS="-m 0 -a /usr/local/bind/dev/log"
```

Now we need to set fairly granular access rights to the directories in the chroot. The daemon will be writing to, reading from, and monitoring the contents of a couple of files under `/usr/local/bind/named`, which contains the zone files for the daemon. We'll grant it the right to read and write to things in that directory but keep it fairly restricted outside of that, even using `chattr` to add the immutable flag to several directories. This keeps those directories from being altered until root removes the immutable flag. `/usr/local/bind/named/local` will contain several zone files for the daemon dealing with the loopback interface, `lo0` (127.0.0.1). Since these never need to be altered, we'll restrict them from being written to, to keep them safe, and take the same action on the main BIND configuration file, `/usr/local/bind/etc/named.conf`.

```
chown root /usr/local/bind /usr/local/bind/named/local
chmod 700 /usr/local/bind
chown dns:dns /usr/local/bind/named
```

```
chmod 700 /usr/local/bind/named
chmod 755 /usr/local/bind/named/local
chmod 444 /usr/local/bind/named/local/*
chown root /usr/local/bind/etc/named.conf
chmod 644 /usr/local/bind/etc/named.conf
chattr +i /usr/local/bind/etc/localtime /usr/local/bind/etc /usr/local/bind/var
chattr +i /usr/local/bind/etc/named.conf /usr/local/bind/named/local/*
```

When the server does not have the answer to a query cached, it must either forward the query to another server or begin making inquiries of its own to discover the information it needs. If you choose the latter approach, the server will need to know where the root servers for the Internet are in order to begin its inquiry by asking those servers where to find the information it needs. You can obtain an up-to-the-minute (not that the information changes that often) copy of the list of these servers from the Internic: fetch `ftp://rs.internic.net/` `domain/named.cache` and you'll have what you need. Once you have it, place that file in `/usr/local/bind/named` so the server can find it, and restrict the permissions on it to prevent attackers from poisoning your cache.

```
cd /usr/local/bind/named
chown root:root /usr/local/bind/named/named.cache
chmod 444 /usr/local/bind/named/named.cache
chattr +i /usr/local/bind/named/named.cache
```

3.4.1.3 Create and Edit Main Configuration File

Now we need to create the main configuration file for the BIND server, `/usr/local/bind/etc/named.conf` (which will become `/etc/` `named.conf` once the server is chrooted). The contents of this file are below: comments in the file may start with a pound (#) sign, or with double slashes (//).

named.conf
```
#
# named.conf file for caching-only DNS server
#


# First we'll establish some ACL groups that define trusted and
# untrusted networks and hosts for certain actions, then we can
# use those throughout the rest of the file as shorthand.
```

```
# This server has no need to perform or receive zone transfers,
# so restrict those completely
acl "xfer" {
none;
};


# This is our internal network, to be trusted to perform certain
# actions such as issuing queries to the server.
acl "trustednets" {
1.3.5.0/24;
};


# These are networks that do not exist. It includes the multicast
# subnets, the subnets defined as "private" by RFC 1918 and the loopback
# network. These should not be seen as source IPs at your server under
# normal circumstances, unless you're using one of the RFC 1918 subnets
# for your internal network. In that case, be sure to block it out of
# this list or the daemon may not accept queries from it!
acl "invalidnets" {
  10.0.0.0/8;
  127.0.0.0/8;
  169.254.0.0/16;
  172.16.0.0/12;
  192.168.0.0/16;
  222.0.0.0/8;
  223.0.0.0/8;
  224.0.0.0/3;
};


options {
  // Remember that all directory paths in this section
  // must be presented relative to the chroot hierarchy!
  // Set the named directory
  directory "/named";
```

```
// Declare the pid-file location for starts and stops
pid-file "/var/run/named.pid";
statistics-file "/var/run/general.stats";
// Memory statistics are not implemented (yet) for v9.2.1
// memstatistics-file "/var/run/memory.stats";
dump-file "/var/run/named.dump";
zone-statistics yes;
// Designate listening interface: listen on the primary adapter
// and the loopback adapter
listen-on { 1.3.5.50; 127.0.0.1; };
// Do not check for interface link state, since it is not a dialup adapter
interface-interval 0;
// Specify an external forwarder, where applicable
        // This is where you would specify to forward queries that are not
        // found in the local cache upstream to other servers.
// forwarders { 3.5.7.10; };
// Permit queries from trusted nets only via "trusted" ACL
allow-query { trustednets; };
// Use "xfer" ACL to define allowed zone transfers (none)
allow-transfer { xfer; };
// Lock out bogus networks using the "invalidnets" ACL
blackhole { invalidnets; };
// Set version string to something non-revealing
// This is a quick fix solution to an query that will reveal the
// version of BIND your server is running, allowing an attacker to
// tailor attacks accordingly. Setting the version string here will
// not log attempts to query this information however, which might
// prove useful from an attack detection standpoint. A slightly more
// complex fix is implemented below, which will log these attempts;
// should you choose not to employ it, simply comment those lines and
// uncomment this one.
// version { "No version here"; };
};
```

```
// Now we need to establish how the server will log information logging {
  channel "default_syslog" {
        // By default, use syslog for logging
        syslog local5;
        severity debug;
  };
  channel "audit_log" {
        // Segregate security-related messages to a separate log file
        file "/usr/local/bind/var/security.log";
        severity debug;
        // Include a timestamp
        print-time yes;
  };
  category default { default_syslog; };
  category general { default_syslog; };
  category security { audit_log; default_syslog; };
  category config { default_syslog; };
  category resolver { audit_log; };
  category xfer-in { audit_log; };
  category xfer-out { audit_log; };
  category notify { audit_log; };
  category client { audit_log; };
  category network { audit_log; };
  category update { audit_log; };
  category queries { audit_log; };
  category lame-servers { audit_log; };
};


// Access view for trusted networks
// This tells the server how to handle queries from internal networks.
view "trusted-query" in {
    // This view will be used for queries matching the "trusted-nets" ACL
    match-clients { trustednets; };
    recursion yes;
```

```
additional-from-auth yes;
additional-from-cache yes;

        // Enable caching of DNS information
        zone "." in {
                type hint;
                file "named.cache";
        };

        // Permit queries for the localhost network, for which
        // every server must be a master
        zone "0.0.127.in-addr.arpa" in {
                type master;
                file "local/reverse.127.0.0";
                allow-query { any; };
                allow-transfer { none; };
        };
};


// Access view for "chaos" records
// This is an old trick but still valid: "chaos" records allow remote machines
// to query the version string from a DNS server running BIND software (they're
// a type of legacy record no longer really used any more). With the following
// settings, we establish a "chaos" record in the zone file local/chaos that
// establishes a completely different set of version and authoring information
// for BIND, and then prevent any queries against it from anywhere, thus creating
// two layers of security. In addition, any queries made against these records
// will be logged by the daemon, because they will get flagged as not allowed.
view "attempt-chaos" chaos {
        match-clients { any; };
        recursion no;

        // Send back empty replies to queries for other CHAOS records
        zone "." {
```

```
                    type hint;
                    file "/dev/null";
        };


            // Prevent anyone from making queries against our special CHAOS records.
            zone "bind" {
                    type master;
                    file "local/chaos";
                    // You may choose to change the "allow-query" field to "trusted",
                    // permitting trusted hosts the right to query your server for its
                    // version information. This can be handy for keeping track of
                    // the software versions on your DNS servers, but treat it carefully!
                    // If you choose to do that, you should alter the local/chaos file
                    // to contain the correct version string, possibly with additional
                    // comments for your admins.
                    allow-query { none; };
                    allow-transfer { none; };
            };
        };
```

You'll need to create some zone files as well: `/usr/local/bind/named/local/chaos` and `/usr/local/bind/named/local/reverse.127.0.0`. Examples of these files appear at the end of this document.

3.4.1.4 Check Configuration Files for Syntax Errors

BIND provides us with a pair of tools that will permit us to check our configuration files for validity before deploying them: this ensures that no one has left out a stray }: anywhere. First, check the main configuration file for errors using `named-checkconf`. We'll have to specify the chroot directory (`-t /usr/local/bind`) and the name of the configuration file as it's seen once the server is chrooted (`/etc/named.conf`):

```
/usr/local/bind/sbin/named-checkconf -t /usr/local/bind /etc/named.conf
```

Now check each of the zone files, using the following syntax:

```
/usr/local/bind/sbin/named-checkzone 0.0.127.in-addr.arpa /usr/local/bind/named/local/
```

You should see in response:

```
zone 0.0.127.in-addr.arpa/IN: loaded serial 42
OK
```

Note that the serial number will vary according to what's in the zone file. Now check the chaos zone we're using (if you've opted to use it):

```
/usr/local/bind/sbin/named-checkzone -c chaos bind /usr/local/bind/named/local/chaos
```

You should see in response:

```
zone bind/CH: loaded serial 42
OK
```

3.4.1.5 Start Daemon with Chroot Manually and Test Lookups

Test that everything is working by manually loading the server and testing to ensure you can look up records. You may need to connect your system to the network at this point if you want to verify that you can look up actual Internet records.

```
/usr/local/bind/sbin/named -u dns -t /usr/local/bind -c /etc/named.conf
```

You can test the server by specifying it on the command line as a second argument to the host command (note that "nslookup" is deprecated, and may be removed from future releases of BIND, so now's the time to get in the habit of using something else instead!):

```
host 127.0.0.1 1.3.5.50
```

You should see in response:

```
Using domain server:
Name: 1.3.5.50
Address: 1.3.5.50#53
Aliases:

1.0.0.127.in-addr.arpa domain name pointer localhost
```

3.4.1.6 Create Startup Files and Add to rc.d Hierarchy

Copy the sample `named` startup script that appears at the end of this section to `/etc/init.d` (or write your own), and add it into the startup hierarchy using `chkconfig`:

```
/sbin/chkconfig —level 2345 —add named
```

3.4.2 Zone Hosting Service

This configuration will differ only a little from the previous, so comments have been included only where commands or instructions differ from what's been provided above. The primary difference with this configuration is that this server will not cache entries: its only job is to answer queries from other servers for domains it knows about, but not to make recursive queries to other servers. This server might live on a DMZ and be exposed to the Internet for incoming queries about the domains it hosts, and thus should never be simultaneously used to query out to the Internet for other domains on behalf of clients. This separation of duties will help keep attacks on your primary nameservers from affecting your inbound clients, possibly subjecting them to cache poisoning attacks that could lead to further breaches.

Many organizations choose to layer their DNS servers with a core DNS server that is configured as primary for all of the organization's domains. This master server is never exposed to the Internet, however: it will answer queries only from the perimeter DNS servers controlled by the organizations. These perimeter hosts are then *configured* to be secondary servers (they perform zone transfers against the master) but are *listed* on the Internet as primary for the organization: machines on the Internet will query them for information about the organization's domains. This setup can help minimize the damage from an attack, since the compromised secondary can be replaced with a duplicate machine and simply instructed to zone-transfer its information from the master, allowing it to be placed in service more quickly. This also means that an attack that changes a record will only do so on the secondary server: the change will be overwritten by the next zone transfer that occurs.

3.4.2.1 Unpack Sources and Compile

```
tar -zxvf bind-9.2.1.tar.gz
cd bind-9.2.1
mkdir /usr/local/bind

./configure —with-openssl —with-randomdev=/dev/random
make
make install DESTDIR=/usr/local/bind
```

3.4.2.2 Set Up Chroot Jail Environment

```
cd /usr/local/bind
```

Notice the addition of the master and slave directories to contain zone files: `master` will contain zone files for domains for which this is the primary DNS server, and `slave` will contain the files for those domains for which this is a secondary server.

```
mkdir -p dev etc named/local named/master named/slave var/run
```

```
useradd -s /dev/null -d /usr/local/bind dns
groupadd dns
```

In order to facilitate zone transfers, the server will need to be able to write zones into the `slave` directory, and to make changes to those files when adding or removing entries as a result of a zone transfer.

```
chown -R dns:dns /usr/local/bind/named/slave
chown -R dns:dns /usr/local/bind/named/var/run
```

```
mknod /usr/local/bind/dev/null c 1 3
mknod /usr/local/bind/dev/random c 1 8
chmod 666 /usr/local/bind/dev/null /usr/local/bind/dev/random
cp /lib/libcrypto.so.2 /usr/local/bind/lib
cp /lib/libnsl.so.1 /usr/local/bind/lib
cp /lib/libc.so.6 /usr/local/bind/lib
cp /lib/libdl.so.2 /usr/local/bind/lib
cp /lib/ld-linux.so.2 /usr/local/bind/lib
cp /etc/localtime /usr/local/bind/etc
```

```
edit /etc/sysconfig/syslog:
  SYSLOGD_OPTIONS="-m 0"
  becomes
  SYSLOGD_OPTIONS="-m 0 -a /usr/local/bind/dev/log"
```

```
chown root /usr/local/bind /usr/local/bind/named/local
```

```
chmod 700 /usr/local/bind
chown dns:dns /usr/local/bind/named
chmod 700 /usr/local/bind/named
chmod 755 /usr/local/bind/named/local
chmod 444 /usr/local/bind/named/local/*
chown root /usr/local/bind/etc/named.conf
chmod 644 /usr/local/bind/etc/named.conf
chattr +i /usr/local/bind/etc/localtime /usr/local/bind/etc /usr/local/bind/var
chattr +i /usr/local/bind/etc/named.conf /usr/local/bind/named/local/*


chattr +i /usr/local/bind/etc/named.conf /usr/local/bind/named/local/*
```

3.4.2.3 Create and Edit Main Configuration File

```
named.conf
  #
  # named.conf file for zone hosting DNS server
  #
  // Permit zone transfers from trusted hosts. Most organizations choose to have
  // another organization host a secondary replica of their zone information, so that in the event
  // of a catastrophe, their servers' information will still be available to the
  // Internet from someone else.
  acl "xfer" {
    2.4.6.5;
  };

  acl "trustednets" {
    1.3.5.0/24;
  };

  acl "invalidnets" {
    10.0.0.0/8;
    127.0.0.0/8;
    169.254.0.0/16;
```

```
      172.16.0.0/12;
      192.168.0.0/16;
      222.0.0.0/8;
      223.0.0.0/8;
      224.0.0.0/3;
   };

   options {
      // Remember that all directory paths in this section
      // must be presented relative to the chroot hierarchy!
      // Set the named directory
      directory "/named";
      // Declare the pid-file location for starts and stops
      pid-file "/var/run/named.pid";
      statistics-file "/var/run/general.stats";
      // memstatistics-file "/var/run/memory.stats";
      dump-file "/var/run/named.dump";
      zone-statistics yes;
      // Designate listening interface
      listen-on { 1.3.5.50; };
      // Do not check for interface link state, since it is not a dialup adapter
      interface-interval 0;
      // Permit queries from trusted nets only via "trusted" ACL
      // If this is a primary server for your domains on the Internet, this will
      // need to change to "any".
      allow-query { trustednets; };
      // Use "xfer" ACL to define allowed zone transfers
      allow-transfer { xfer; };
      // Lock out bogus networks using the "invalidnets" ACL
      blackhole { invalidnets; };
      // Set version string to something non-revealing — this will not log attempts
      // to query CHAOS information, however.
      // version { "No version here"; };
   };
```

```
logging {
 channel "default_syslog" {
  // Default logging to syslog
  syslog local5;
  severity debug;
 };
 channel "audit_log" {
  // Segregate security messages to a separate log
  file "/var/run/security.log";
  severity debug;
  // Include a timestamp
  print-time yes;
 };
 category default { default_syslog; };
 category general { default_syslog; };
 category security { audit_log; default_syslog; };
 category config { default_syslog; };
 category resolver { audit_log; };
 category xfer-in { audit_log; };
 category xfer-out { audit_log; };
 category notify { audit_log; };
 category client { audit_log; };
 category network { audit_log; };
 category update { audit_log; };
 category queries { audit_log; };
 category lame-servers { audit_log; };
};


// Create the access view for internal trusted networks
// Here, we're creating the first of two "views" of the data on this server. This one
// will present different information to internal clients than to external clients, a
// configuration known colloquially as "split-brain DNS". ISC recommends splitting
// this configuration up into a separate internal and external DNS server, but not
// every organization can afford two machines for this. If that's the case, this
```

```
// split configuration will come in handy. If you can afford two machines, you can
// divide this configuration up and use this internal view for your internal DNS server
// and the external view below for the external.
view "trusted-query" in {
 match-clients { trustednets; };
 // Remember that this server is not caching at all: that should be the job of a
 // separate machine in your organization, for security and performance reasons,
 // particularly if this machine is already doing double duty presenting internal
 // and external DNS information to both sets of clients. If you need this machine
 // to also cache DNS queries and forward them on behalf of your clients, turn on
 // the "forwarders" option in the options{} block above, and set "recursion" and
 // "additional-from-cache" to "yes" below. Then activate the caching "hint" block
 // below.
 recursion no;
 additional-from-auth yes;
 additional-from-cache no;

    // Enable the cache — disabled since this machine is not caching.
    // zone "." in {
         // type hint;
         // file "named.cache";
    // };

    // Permit queries for the localhost network, for which
    // every server must be a master
    zone "0.0.127.in-addr.arpa" in {
         type master;
         file "local/reverse.127.0.0";
         allow-query { any; };
         allow-transfer { none; };
    };

    // Send internal-only data to trusted internal networks
    zone "example.com" in {
```

```
                type master;
                file "master/example.com_internal";
        };


        // Don't forget reverse records
        zone "5.3.1.in-addr.arpa" in {
                type master;
                file "master/reverse.1.3.5";
        };

};

view "external-query" in {
  match-clients { any; };
  recursion no;
  additional-from-auth no;
  additional-from-cache no;
    // Enable the cache
    zone "." in {
                type hint;
                file "named.cache";
        };


        // Permit queries for the localhost network, for which
        // every server must be a master
        zone "0.0.127.in-addr.arpa" in {
                type master;
                file "local/reverse.127.0.0";
                allow-query { any; };
                allow-transfer { none; };
        };


        // Send external data only
        zone "mydomain.com" in {
```

```
            type master;
            file "master/mydomain.com_external";
            allow-query { any; };
        };


        // Send reverse records for external subnet
        zone "6.4.2.in-addr.arpa" in {
            type master;
            file "master/reverse.2.4.6";
            allow-query { any; };
        };
    };


    view "attempt-chaos" chaos {
        match-clients { any; };
        recursion no;
        zone "." {
            type hint;
            file "/dev/null";
        };


        zone "bind" {
            type master;
            file "local/chaos";
            allow-query { none; };
            allow-transfer { none; };
        };
    };
```

3.4.2.4 Check Configuration Files for Syntax Errors

BIND provides us with a pair of tools that will permit us to check our configuration files for validity before deploying them: this ensures that no one has left out a stray }: anywhere. First, check the main configuration file for errors using `named-checkconf`. We'll have to specify the chroot directory

(`-t /usr/local/bind`) and the name of the configuration file as it's seen once the server is chrooted (`/etc/named.conf`):

```
/usr/local/bind/sbin/named-checkconf -t /usr/local/bind /etc/named.conf
```

Now check each of the zone files, using the following syntax:

```
/usr/local/bind/sbin/named-checkzone 0.0.127.in-addr.arpa /usr/local/bind/named/local/
```

You should see in response:

```
zone 0.0.127.in-addr.arpa/IN: loaded serial 42
OK
```

Note that the serial number will vary according to what's in the zone file. Repeat this process for each of the other zone files you've created.

Finally, check the chaos zone we're using, if you've opted to use it:

```
/usr/local/bind/sbin/named-checkzone -c chaos bind /usr/local/bind/named/local/chaos
```

You should see in response:

```
zone bind/CH: loaded serial 42
OK
```

3.4.2.5 Start Daemon with Chroot Manually and Test Lookups

Test that everything is working by manually loading the server and testing to ensure you can look up records. You may need to connect your system to the network at this point if you want to verify that you can look up actual Internet records.

```
/usr/local/bind/sbin/named -u dns -t /usr/local/bind -c /etc/named.conf
```

You can test the server by specifying it on the command line as a second argument to the host command (note that "nslookup" is deprecated, and may be removed from future releases of BIND, so now's the time to get in the habit of using something else instead!):

```
host 127.0.0.1 1.3.5.50
```

You should see in response:

```
Using domain server:
Name: 1.3.5.50
Address: 1.3.5.50#53
Aliases:


1.0.0.127.in-addr.arpa domain name pointer localhost
```

3.4.2.6 Create Startup Files and Add to rc.d Hierarchy

Copy the sample `named` startup script that appears at the end of this section to `/etc/init.d` (or write your own), and add it into the startup hierarchy using `chkconfig`:

```
/sbin/chkconfig —level 2345 —add named
```

3.4.3 Sample BIND Configuration Files

/usr/local/bind/named/local/chaos
```
$TTL    1D
$ORIGIN bind.
@ CHAOS SOA localhost. root.localhost. (
        42    ; serial
        3H    ; refresh
        15M   ; retry
        1W    ; expiry
        1D )  ; minimum
@ CHAOS NS  localhost.


version.bind. CH  TXT "No version here"
authors.bind. CH  TXT "No authors here"
```

/usr/local/bind/named/local/reverse.127.0.0
```
$TTL    1D
$ORIGIN     0.0.127.in-addr.arpa
@ 1D IN SOA localhost. root.localhost. (
        42    ; serial
```

```
        3H    ; refresh
        15M   ; retry
        1W    ; expiry
        1D )  ; minimum
    1D   IN NS  localhost.
  1 1D   IN PTR localhost.
```

/usr/local/bind/named/local/localhost

```
    $TTL 1D
    @ 1D IN SOA @ root.localhost. (
            42    ; serial
            3H    ; refresh
            15M   ; retry
            1W    ; expiry
            1D )  ; minimum
      1D   IN NS @
    1 1D   IN A 127.0.0.1
```

/usr/local/bind/named/master/mydomain.com_internal

```
    $TTL 1D
    @ 1D IN SOA @ root.mydomain.com. (
            42    ; serial
            3H    ; refresh
            15M   ; retry
            1W    ; expiry
            1D )  ; minimum
      1D    IN NS @
    ns      IN A 1.3.5.50
   www      IN A 1.3.5.20
```

/usr/local/bind/named/master/mydomain_external

```
    $TTL 1D
    @ 1D IN SOA @ root.mydomain.com. (
            42    ; serial
```

```
        3H    ; refresh
        15M   ; retry
        1W    ; expiry
        1D )  ; minimum
    1D    IN NS @
ns        IN A 2.4.6.5
www       IN A 2.4.6.20
```

/usr/local/bind/named/master/reverse.1.3.5

```
    $TTL 1D
    $ORIGIN 5.3.1.in-addr.arpa
    @ 1D IN SOA mydomain.com. root.mydomain.com. (
            42   ; serial
            3H    ; refresh
            15M   ; retry
            1W    ; expiry
            1D )  ; minimum
    1D    IN NS ns.
20        IN PTR www.
50        IN PTR ns.
```

/usr/local/bind/named/master/reverse.2.4.6

```
    $TTL 1D
    $ORIGIN 6.4.2.in-addr.arpa
    @ 1D IN SOA localhost. root.localhost. (
            42   ; serial
            3H    ; refresh
            15M   ; retry
            1W    ; expiry
            1D )  ; minimum
    1D    IN NS ns.
5         IN PTR ns.
20        IN PTR www.
```

/etc/init.d/named

```sh
#!/bin/sh
# named This file will start and stop the BIND named daemon
#
# chkconfig: 2345 99 99
# description: named is the daemon responsible for mapping IP addresses \
# to names and vice versa in response to queries from other hosts.
# processname: /usr/local/bind/sbin/named
# config: /usr/local/bind/etc/named.conf

# Source function library
. /etc/rc.d/init.d/functions

# Source networking functionality and ensure that the network has been started
if [ -f /etc/sysconfig/network ]; then
  . /etc/sysconfig/network
  [ ${NETWORKING} = "no" ] && exit 0
fi

[ -x /usr/local/bind/sbin/named ] || exit 0

RETVAL=0
prog="named"

# Set variables for the chroot
CHROOT_USER=dns
CHROOT_DIR=/usr/local/bind
CHROOT_CONFIG=/etc/named.conf

start() {
  echo -n $"Starting $prog: "
  daemon /usr/local/bind/sbin/named -u $CHROOT_USER -t $CHROOT_DIR -c $CHROOT_CONFIG
  RETVAL=$?
  echo
```

```
  touch /var/lock/subsys/named
  return $RETVAL
}

stop() {
  echo -n $"Stopping $prog: "
  killproc /usr/local/bind/sbin/named
  RETVAL=$?
  echo
  rm -f /var/lock/subsys/named
  return $RETVAL
}

restart() {
  stop
  start
}

reload() {
  /usr/local/bind/sbin/ndc reload
}

condrestart() {
  [ -e /var/lock/subsys/named ] && restart
  return 0
}

case "$1" in
  start)
    start
    ;;
  stop)
    stop
    ;;
```

```
   restart)
     restart
     ;;
   reload)
     reload
     ;;
   condrestart)
     condrestart
     ;;
   status)
     status named
     RETVAL=$?
     ;;
   *)
     echo $"Usage: $0 {start|stop|status|restart|condrestart|reload}"
     RETVAL=1
     ;;
esac

exit $RETVAL
```

4.1 SWATCH

Swatch (The Simple WATCHer) is a popular open source log monitoring and alerting utility written by Todd Atkins. Swatch is designed to monitor your log files against a set of configurable triggers. When Swatch detects a triggered event, it can alert the system administrator via the console, an audible beep, or an e-mail. In addition to real-time monitoring of log files, Swatch can also be used to filter old log files for suspected activity. Swatch can be obtained at http://www.oit.ucsb.edu/~eta/swatch/

4.2 TRIPWIRE

Tripwire is a file integrity application that is available both commercially and as an open-source product for Linux. Tripwire works by creating a hash for all files that you have chosen to monitor on your system. These hashes are then stored in a database. Once the database is created you can schedule tripwire to run on a regular basis to compare the hashes of the files you were monitoring to the hashes stored in the database. The main advantages to the commercial version are vendor support and the availability of a centralized management console. The commercial version of tripwire can be obtained at www.tripwire.com. The open source version of tripwire can be obtained at www.tripwire.org.

4.3 INTRUSION DETECTION SYSTEMS

Intrusion Detection Systems (IDS) are a hot topic in security circles today. These security devices are designed to monitor networks for suspected malicious activity. Once this activity is detected, the device sends an alert to an administrator and in some cases can even respond to the event based on pre-configured options. With major players like Cisco, ISS and Symantec providing IDS solutions, the cost for a commercial Intrusion Detection System can be considerable. This cost factor has influenced many small companies and some larger companies to implement an open source IDS solution known as SNORT. SNORT is a lightweight intrusion detection system that provides many of the same features as commercial IDSs. The security community has also developed many open source add-ons, such as management consoles and reporting tools, for SNORT. Because of this, SNORT can perform just as well as any commercial system while providing considerable cost savings. Some IDS solutions that run on the Linux platform include:

ISS Realsecure – http://www.iss.net
Enterasys Dragon – http://www.enterasys.com
SNORT – http://www.snort.org

4.4 JOHN THE RIPPER

John the Ripper is a freeware password auditing utility or, as some like to call it, a password cracking utility. John the Ripper attempts to brute force guess the passwords in the passwd and shadow files, making use of dictionaries and its knowledge of common password creation techniques. John the Ripper has three modes in which it will run:

- Single Crack Mode – Uses the login and GECOS (Full Name, home directory, etc) information from the passwd file as its password word list.
- Wordlist Mode – Uses a populated wordlist or dictionary list.
- Incremental Mode – Uses all combinations of characters. This is sometimes known as brute force mode.

John the Ripper can be obtained at http://www.openwall.com/john/.

4.5 CRACK

Crack is another freeware password auditing utility. Similar to John the Ripper, in order to use crack you need to combine your passwd and shadow files. By default crack uses wordlists. For a brute force scan of a password file you would use crack7, which is included with the install of crack. Crack can be obtained at http://packetstorm.decepticons.org/Crackers/crack/.

4.6 BASTILLE

Bastille is a Linux hardening application that provides novice and experienced users a way to automate many of the security settings that have been covered in this guide. Bastille provides both a command line and GUI format for users. Bastille walks the user through an interactive questionnaire to determine which setting should be turned on and what the ramifications are for making those changes. Bastille can be obtained at http://www.bastille-linux.org/.

4.7 NMAP

NMAP or Network Mapper is an excellent freeware reconnaissance utility. NMAP is typically used as a port mapper utility, sending packets to hosts with various settings to determine which ports are open on a device. NMAP can also be used as an Operating System reconnaissance tool since NMAP has the ability to send packets to a host and, based on the response to those packets, determine which Operating System the host is running. NMAP can be obtained at www.nmap.org.

4.8 NESSUS

Nessus is a freeware vulnerability assessment tool. Nessus works on a client/server based technology. The server side contains the vulnerability database and the engine that actually performs the vulnerability assessment. The client connects to the server to configure the settings for the vulnerability assessment. Nessus can provide reports in a number of different formats including its native GUI format, HTML, and ASCII. Nessus can be obtained at www.nessus.org.

4.9 PSIONIC PORTSENTRY

Psionic PortSentry, a freeware tool that is part of a suite of tools called the TriSentry Suite, is designed to detect and respond to portscans against a host machine. PortSentry has the ability to detect port scans coming into a system and then to dynamically block access to the scanning systems using kernel routing tables, kernel firewalling, tcp wrappers, or a custom command of your choosing. LogSentry, another freeware log monitoring tool, can monitor your logs for configurable activities and send alerts based on that configuration. Both LogSentry and PortSentry can be obtained at www.psionic.com.

Security Resources

Center for Internet Security – http://www.cisecurity.org

DNS Security – http://www.isc.org/products/BIND

Hacking Linux Exposed: Firewalling /proc Entries – http://www.hackinglinuxexposed.com/articles/20021015.html

Linux Security – http://www.linuxsecurity.com

SANS – http://www.sans.org

Security Focus – http://www.securityfocus.org

Security Tracker – http://www.securitytracker.com

Securing Apache Step by Step – http://www.giac.org/practical/ryan_barnett_gcux.zip

Red Hat Resources

Red Hat – http://www.redhat.com

Red Hat Advisories - https://rhn.redhat.com/errata/rh73-errata.html

Red Hat Docs – http://www.redhat.com/docs/manuals/RHNetwork/ref-guide/)

Red Hat Mirrors – http://www.redhat.com/mirrors

Third Party Resources

APACHE – http://httpd.apache.org

APACHE MODS– http://httpd.apache.org/docs/mod/

AUTORPM – http://www.autorpm.org

BASTILLE – http://www.bastille-linux.org

EXIM – http://www.exim.org

IMAP Connection, The – http://www.imap.org/

IPTABLES – http://www.iptables.org

JOHN THE RIPPER – http://www.openwall.com/john/

LOGWATCH – http://www.logwatch.org

NESSUS – http://www.nessus.org

NMAP – http://www.nmap.org

NTP – http://www.cis.udel.edu/~ntp

OPENSSH – http://www.openssh.com

OPENSSH – http://www.openssh.org/portable.html

PSIONIC TRISENTRY – http://www.psionic.com

POSTFIX – http://www.postfix.org

QMAIL – http://www.qmail.org

QPOPPER – http://www.eudora.com/qpopper/

SAMBA – http://www.samba.org/

SENDMAIL – http://www.sendmail.org

SNMP – http://www.snmplink.org

SNORT – http://www.snort.org

SWATCH – http://www.oit.ucsb.edu/~eta/swatch/

Time Servers – http://www.eecis.udel.edu/~mills/ntp/servers.html

TRIPWIRE – http://www.tripwire.org

WU-FTP – http://www.wu-ftpd.org

XINETD – http://www.xinetd.org

1. /etc/security/access.conf

```
# Login access control table.
#
# When someone logs in, the table is scanned for the first entry that
# matches the (user, host) combination, or, in case of non-networked
# logins, the first entry that matches the (user, tty) combination. The
# permissions field of that table entry determines whether the login will
# be accepted or refused.
#
# Format of the login access control table is three fields separated by a
# ":" character:
#
#         permission : users : origins
#
# The first field should be a "+" (access granted) or "-" (access denied)
# character.
#
# The second field should be a list of one or more login names, group
# names, or ALL (always matches). A pattern of the form user@host is
# matched when the login name matches the "user" part, and when the
# "host" part matches the local machine name.
#
# The third field should be a list of one or more tty names (for
# non-networked logins), host names, domain names (begin with "."), host
# addresses, internet network numbers (end with "."), ALL (always
# matches) or LOCAL (matches any string that does not contain a "."
# character).
#
# If you run NIS you can use @netgroupname in host or user patterns; this
# even works for @usergroup@@hostgroup patterns. Weird.
```

```
#
# The EXCEPT operator makes it possible to write very compact rules.
#
# The group file is searched only when a name does not match that of the
# logged-in user. Both the user's primary group is matched, as well as
# groups in which users are explicitly listed.
#
################################################################################
#
# Disallow console logins to all but a few accounts.
#
#-:ALL EXCEPT wheel shutdown sync:LOCAL
#
# Disallow non-local logins to privileged accounts (group wheel).
#
#-:wheel:ALL EXCEPT LOCAL .win.tue.nl
#
# Some accounts are not allowed to login from anywhere:
#
#-:wsbscaro wsbsecr wsbspac wsbsym wscosor wstaiwde:ALL
#
# All other accounts are allowed to login from anywhere.
#
```

2. /etc/security/limits.conf

```
# /etc/security/limits.conf
#
#Each line describes a limit for a user in the form:
#
#<domain> <type> <item> <value>
#
#Where:
#<domain> can be:
```

```
#             - a user name
#             - a group name, with @group syntax
#             - the wildcard *, for default entry
#
#<type> can have the two values:
#             - "soft" for enforcing the soft limits
#             - "hard" for enforcing hard limits
#
#<item> can be one of the following:
#             - core - limits the core file size (KB)
#             - data - max data size (KB)
#             - fsize - maximum filesize (KB)
#             - memlock - max locked-in-memory address space (KB)
#             - nofile - max number of open files
#             - rss - max resident set size (KB)
#             - stack - max stack size (KB)
#             - cpu - max CPU time (MIN)
#             - nproc - max number of processes
#             - as - address space limit
#             - maxlogins - max number of logins for this user
#             - priority - the priority to run user process with
#             - locks - max number of file locks the user can hold
#
#<domain>          <type>      <item>        <value>
#


#*                 soft        core          0
#*                 hard        rss           10000
#@student          hard        nproc         20
#@faculty          soft        nproc         20
#@faculty          hard        nproc         50
#ftp               hard        nproc         0
#@student          -           maxlogins     4
```

```
# End of file
```

3. /etc/security/time.conf

```
# this is an example configuration file for the pam_time module. Its syntax
# was initially based heavily on that of the shadow package (shadow-960129).
#
# the syntax of the lines is as follows:
#
#        services;ttys;users;times
#
# white space is ignored and lines maybe extended with '\\n' (escaped
# newlines). As should be clear from reading these comments,
# text following a '#' is ignored to the end of the line.
#
# the combination of individual users/terminals etc is a logic list
# namely individual tokens that are optionally prefixed with '!' (logical
# not) and separated with '&' (logical and) and '|' (logical or).
#
# services
#        is a logic list of PAM service names that the rule applies to.
#
# ttys
#        is a logic list of terminal names that this rule applies to.
#
# users
#        is a logic list of users to whom this rule applies.
#
#NB. For these items the simple wildcard '*' may be used only once.
#
# times
#        the format here is a logic list of day/time-range
#        entries the days are specified by a sequence of two character
```

```
#          entries, MoTuSa for example is Monday Tuesday and Saturday. Note
#          that repeated days are unset MoMo = no day, and MoWk = all weekdays
#          bar Monday. The two character combinations accepted are
#
#               Mo Tu We Th Fr Sa Su Wk Wd Al
#
#          the last two being week-end days and all 7 days of the week
#          respectively. As a final example, AlFr means all days except Friday.
#
#          each day/time-range can be prefixed with a '!' to indicate "anything
#          but"
#
#          The time-range part is two 24-hour times HHMM separated by a hyphen
#          indicating the start and finish time (if the finish time is smaller
#          than the start time it is deemed to apply on the following day).
#
# for a rule to be active, ALL of service+ttys+users must be satisfied
# by the applying process.
#


#
# Here is a simple example: running blank on tty* (any ttyXXX device),
# the users 'you' and 'me' are denied service all of the time
#

#blank;tty* & !ttyp*;you|me;!Al0000-2400

# Another silly example, user 'root' is denied xsh access
# from pseudo terminals at the weekend and on mondays.

#xsh;ttyp*;root;!WdMo0000-2400


#
```

```
# End of example file.
#
```

4. /etc/syslog.conf

```
#############
# Section 1: For all system (servers and workstations)
#############
# Log all info or higher messages, except facilities that use their own log
*.info;authpriv,auth,mail,cron,kern,local7.none          /var/log/messages

# authpriv is intended for messages related to authorizations
# (e.g. failed login attempts). auth is deprecated, but included
# in case some older programs still use it.
authpriv,auth.*                                          /var/log/secure

# Send mail messages to a separate file.
mail.*                                                   /var/log/maillog

# Send crond and atd messages to a separate file.
cron.*                                                   /var/log/cron

# Send kernel messages to a separate file. Note that this will
# include messages generated by iptables about blocked network traffic.
kern.*                                                   /var/log/kernel

# Send boot messages to a separate file
local7.*                                                 /var/log/boot.log

# Send emergency messages of any type to all logged in users
*.emerg                                                          *

#############
# If you have a remote logging host, uncomment the lines corresponding to
```

```
# the types of messages you want to forward to it. Replace the string
# loghost with the IP address of your central logging server.
#############

#kern.*                  @loghost
#authpriv,auth.*         @loghost
#mail.*                  @loghost


#############
# Section 2: For servers only
#############

# If this is an FTP server, uncomment the next line and add ftp to
# the comma-separated list of facilities sent to the messages file.
# ftp.*                                  /var/log/ftp

# If this is a NEWS server, uncomment the next line and add news to
# the comma-separated list of facilities sent to the messages file.
# news.*                                 /var/log/news

# If this is a print server, uncomment the next line and add lpr to
# the comma-separated list of facilities sent to the messages file.
# lpr.*                                  /var/log/spooler
```